STOP
TEACHING
OUR KIDS
TO KILL

Revised and Updated Edition

ALSO BY LT. COL. DAVE GROSSMAN

*On Killing: The Psychological Cost of
Learning to Kill in War and Society*

*On Combat: The Psychology and Physiology of
Deadly Conflict in War and in Peace*
(with Loren W. Christensen)

ALSO BY GLORIA DeGAETANO

Left to Their Devices, What's Left?

*Parenting Well in a Media Age:
Keeping Our Kids Human*

STOP TEACHING OUR KIDS TO KILL

Revised and Updated Edition

A CALL TO ACTION AGAINST TV, MOVIE & VIDEO GAME VIOLENCE

LT. COL. DAVE GROSSMAN
AND GLORIA DeGAETANO

HARMONY
BOOKS · NEW YORK

Copyright © 1999, 2014 by Dave Grossman and Gloria DeGaetano

Published in the United States by Harmony Books, an imprint of
the Crown Publishing Group, a division of Random House LLC,
a Penguin Random House Company, New York.
www.crownpublishing.com

HARMONY BOOKS is a registered trademark, and the Circle
colophon is a trademark of Random House LLC.

A previous edition was published in hardcover in the United States
by Crown Publishers, an imprint of the Crown Publishing Group,
a division of Random House LLC, New York, in 1999.

Library of Congress Cataloging-in-Publication Data
Grossman, Dave.
Stop teaching our kids to kill: a call to action against TV,
movie & video game violence / by Lt. Col. Dave Grossman
and Gloria DeGaetano.—Revised and updated edition.
pages   cm
Includes bibliographical references and index.
1. Mass media and children. 2. Television and children.
3. Violence on television. 4. Children and violence.
I. DeGaetano, Gloria. II. Title.
HQ784.M3G76   2014
302.230835—dc23   2013050666

ISBN 978-0-8041-3935-9
eBook ISBN 978-0-8041-3936-6

Printed in the United States of America

Jacket design by Michael Nagin

2 4 6 8 10 9 7 5 3 1

Second Edition

To the children of the world

and

to the survival of their innocence

CONTENTS

STOP
TEACHING
OUR KIDS
TO KILL

IT'S NOT NORMAL

The first edition of this book actually began in 1997 over a dinner conversation. We had become familiar with each other's work through a mutual colleague and decided it was time to meet. Dave had written *On Killing: The Psychological Cost of Learning to Kill in War and Society*, which examined the army's conditioning techniques used to overcome soldiers' aversion to killing. Now a classic, *On Killing* showed how media, particularly violent video games, replicate these techniques. Since 1987, Gloria—with no knowledge of Dave's work—had been helping parents and professionals understand the conditioning effects of violent media from the perspective of child and adolescent brain vulnerabilities.

A lively discussion soon uncovered a mutual passion: We wanted parents, educators, law enforcement officers—anyone working with children and youth—to know without equivocation that media violence harms. We wanted to make people aware of how the prolific use of sensational violence in television, movies, and in video games affects kids' attitudes and actions. We wanted to reveal the scientific research on the subject—research that couldn't make clearer the deadly link between violent graphic imagery and the escalating incidence of youth violence. We wanted anyone who cares about kids to understand that media violence is a serious threat to them, and to our society as well.

Now, in this revised 2014 edition, we have the same goals as we did in the original 1999 edition—but with much more urgency. Incredibly, misconceptions and misinformation still abound about media violence, leading to collective confusion and individual inaction. Parents throw up their hands in despair, so frustrated with their kids' video game habits that they have given up. Teachers are at their wits' end with the "culture of cruelty" in their schools. And congressional debates about what to do about media violence come and go while our kids get better at killing. Today it seems inevitable that the kids who gave us Jonesboro in the middle school and Littleton in the high school are now giving us mall massacres, workplace shootings, and college rampages. Why? Because we have not yet done enough to address the root cause of the problem.

And that root cause is the steady diet of violent entertainment our kids see on TV, in movies, and in the video games they play—as they sit in front of their screens and digital devices for forty hours each week. This amount of continuous exposure to gratuitous violent images sensationalizing murder, rape, and torture is neither benign nor cathartic. The fact is that media violence primes children to see killing as acceptable.

Over the years we have heard firsthand many horror stories that show the link between media violence and aggression. Teachers report first graders stabbing kittens to death and mutilating pets after seeing violent acts on TV or in a movie. Parents observe preschoolers attempting to drown siblings because a cartoon hero drowned an enemy on TV. Law enforcement officers tell of the hundreds of preteens who plot murder and revenge and luckily are stopped before the tragedy occurs. Adolescents who copy crimes they see on television do so with cold-blooded calculation and without remorse. They even detect and correct the flaws that may have caused the television crime to fail.

It's abnormal for a civilized society to teach kids to kill people. And it's certainly not normal for so many kids to want to kill, harm, bully, or hurt others as they do today.

We have deterred many violent crimes by putting thousands of armed police officers in our schools. But it seems that we have forgotten that it is not normal to put thousands of cops in our schools to stop our kids from killing each other. And it's not normal for every kid in America to practice hunkering down, hiding under tables when their classmates come to kill them.

In recent years, we also have detected potential youth killers by the hundreds, catching them before they commit their crimes. But once again it is not normal to apprehend hundreds of kids every year who are planning to commit mass murders in our schools. The most fundamental shift in law enforcement tactics in our lifetime happened after Columbine. Today, "Rapid Reaction" and "Active Mass Murder" response programs train officers to go in and stop the killings. And it works. Most people never heard about what happened in the high school in Spokane, Washington, in 2003. The police were in that school in minutes and ultimately shot the suspect before he could take a single life. He survived. (Nobody died that day, so it is not on anybody's "list" of these brutal crimes.) The police who were there said one of the first things out of the shooter's mouth was "How'd you get here so fast?"

Yes, police are good at entering our schools like thunder and shooting wannabe juvenile mass murderers before they can rack up a body count, but it is not normal. We don't know about you, but we are outraged that every police officer in America has to practice going into our schools and shooting our kids. It's *not normal*.

Of course, not every kid will walk into a school and start killing people. But all our children are being damaged by heavy exposure to screen violence and in a variety of ways. As we show in this revised edition, the scientific evidence keeps mounting, demonstrating clearly that kids will become more aggressive, reactive, and increasingly desensitized with increased exposure to media violence. Then who knows? With other risk factors in kids' lives they could become the killer next door.

There is a generation out there that has been fed violence from its youngest days, and has been systematically taught to associate pleasure and reward with vivid depictions of inflicting human death and suffering. These young people are coming to our old folks' homes and our movie theaters. They are coming to our school buses, our kindergarten classes, our Little League games, our hospitals, and our day-care centers. When it happens, never let yourself think it is normal. Never lose your sense of outrage. And never, never let yourself forget—as we will demonstrate in the following chapters—that the violence fed to children in the form of TV, movies, and video games is the new factor causing our kids to kill and to grow into adults who kill and want to kill others.

We believe we can help stop all this. Reading this revised edition you will find pertinent brain science information clearly laid out to address how media violence affects children and adolescents at different ages and stages of development—ages three to five, six to ten, eleven to fourteen, and fifteen to eighteen. We explain other risk factors besides media violence because we know it is never one thing that prompts anyone to kill. We thoroughly detail important protective factors we all can put in kids' lives, doing a better job to immunize them against the harmful effects of media violence. And we give you the latest research and the most current statements by experts against media violence, which you can share with friends and colleagues. In this book, you have everything you need in one place—current research, clear guidelines, practical strate-

gies, and in-depth resources. In effect, we give you a blueprint for effective action to make an important difference
at home, in your community, and in the larger world so
that we can work together to end this problem and create a
safer environment for us all.

With relevant information, practical solutions, and the
will to succeed, we can stop teaching our kids to kill and to
want to kill. We offer you the information and solutions on
the following pages. As for the will, well, that's up to you.

CHAPTER ONE

IT'S A VIOLENT WORLD...
FOR OUR KIDS

Youth today are raised in a culture of death, and murder seems to be something that comes naturally as a way to solve their problems. Something drastic needs to be done to take violence out of our everyday culture.

—Phil Chalmers, *Inside the Mind of a Teen Killer*

Media violence, especially violent video games, came under intense scrutiny after the April 20, 1999, massacre at Columbine High School in Littleton, Colorado. Equipped with guns, knives, and explosives, two senior students, Eric Harris and Dylan Klebold went on a crazed shooting spree, murdering twelve students and one teacher, and injuring twenty-four others.

Harris and Klebold were avid players of the violent video game Doom. Popular in the 1990s, Doom is widely known as an early example of the first-person shooter genre. As the player-perpetrator progressed in the game, he increased his ammunition-carrying capacity until, finally achieving "berserk mode," he inflicted "rocket-launcher level damage." The boys, fascinated with Doom, practiced "going berserk" for hundreds of hours. While planning for the massacre, Harris said that the killing would be "like playing *Doom*." And the rifle he would use would be "straight out of the game." Therefore, it should not be altogether surprising that their bizarre behaviors resembled something out of the cyber world of a typical Doom scenario.

Columbine bears the disturbing distinction of being a watershed moment in U.S. history, "defining the social category of a rampage school shooting." When it occurred, it shook us to our core. We didn't think it could get any worse. But it has. The 2012 tragedy at Newtown, Connecticut, was the first time a shooter entered an elementary school.

On the morning of December 14, 2012, twenty-year-old Adam Lanza, using his mother's rifle, fired four shots into her head, then drove to Sandy Hook Elementary School, where he killed twenty-six people—six adults and twenty children in less than five minutes. Wearing black clothing, earplugs, and an olive green utility vest, he shot his way through a locked glass door at the front of the school. Authorities determined that Lanza shot all of his victims multiple times, and at least one victim, six-year-old Noah Pozner, eleven times. Most of the shooting took place in two first-grade classrooms near the entrance of the school, where he killed fourteen in one room and six in the other. A six-year-old girl, the sole survivor from one of the classrooms said that she stayed alive by playing dead. The child described the shooter as a very angry man.

Lanza, it turns out, like Harris and Klebold thirteen years earlier, was "an extremely active player" of another first-person shooter game. Lanza's choice, Combat Arms, features realistic weapons with the goal of acquiring better ones through repeated play. Lanza's dedication to the game is chilling. He recorded 83,496 "kills," including 22,725 headshots. Headshots indicate mastery achievement in video game play, with extra points given for them. No one, however, gave Lanza extra points for the four bullets he put through his mother's head.

Columbine and Newtown were famous cases. But there have been others—some you may not have heard about. Merely one month after the tragedy at Sandy Hook, fifteen-year-old Nehemiah Griego, a self-admitted "violent video game lover," demonstrated his proficiency with headshots. Just after midnight he walked into his parents' bedroom, where his mother and younger brother were sleeping, and took the rifle from the closet. He then shot his mother, Sara, in the head, and when his nine-year-old brother, Zephania, awoke and said he did not believe she was dead, Nehemiah picked up her head to show him. When Zephania began to cry, Griego shot him dead, too, before going into the room where his five-year-old sister Jael and two-year-old sister Angelina were sleeping. Nehemiah stated he "lost his sense of conscience" and shot both of his crying sisters in the head. Then, impassively, Griego lay in wait for his father to come home from his night job, and ambushed and shot him. The next morning he went to Calvary Church, where his father had once been pastor, and told people his family was dead. He confessed, saying he did it because he was "annoyed with his mother." "Unemotional" when talking about the murders, Griego perked up when asked about the video games he played. Police reported that Griego did not have drugs or alcohol in his system, and there is no indication he was ever treated for mental illness. "This is beyond any human reasoning or understanding," a detective admitted after observing the horrific scene. Yet, Griego's calculated killings and his unemotional reaction are common among kids who kill and who are heavily invested in violent entertainment. Their initial icy determination and numbness afterward mimic the psychopathic attitudes of their video game counterparts.

Kids immersed in violent entertainment can blur lines between reality and fantasy. They really don't know why they commit a horrendous crime. On March 24, 2013, thirteen-year-old Noah Crooks shot his mother twenty times with a .22 caliber rifle and then texted his father, "Dad this is Noah. I killed mom accidentally. I regret it. Come home now please." Logically you can't shoot someone twenty times and call it an accident. But Crooks confused rapidly pulling the real trigger twenty times with the callous, all-out shooting he practiced for up to eighteen hours a day playing violent video games. One of his favorites was the misogynistic, yet extremely popular Grand Theft Auto, which includes killing prostitutes after you have sex with them. On the phone with the 911 dispatcher, he said, "I feel crazy and I know I'm not . . . I tried to rape her. I tried to rape her but I couldn't do it . . . I tried to rape my own mom. Who tries to rape their own mom?"

All Crook's mother had done was take away his video game controller because of his bad grades.

Since they practice murder in the virtual world to the point of obsessiveness, youth weaned on violent video games carry out their slaughter in ways that closely resemble the world that preoccupies them. That's what John Zawahri did on June 10, 2013, when he turned the beachfront community of Santa Monica, California, into a battlefield. Zawahri, age twenty-three, who was once a bomb-making teen, shot at cars and at anyone in sight after killing his father and brother and burning down their house. By the time he finished, six innocent people were dead, including a sixty-eight-year-old woman whom he shot in the head at point-blank range. Eyewitnesses and authorities described the melee as a "copycat of the video game, Grand Theft Auto," complete with house burning and carjacking. "GTA," currently in its fifth iteration, has been notorious for its haphazard mayhem and pointless violence, often set in beachfront communities eerily similar to Santa Monica.

Zawahri isn't the only youth who has mimicked GTA. The version Vice City played a role in the murderous actions of eighteen-year-old Devon Moore, who in 2003 killed two policemen and a dispatcher, then fled in a patrol car, saying, "Life is a video game. Everybody's got to die." In one of the game's episodes there is a mission that depicts exactly what Moore did: escape a police station, kill officers, and flee in a police cruiser.

School shootings and murders by youth and young adults with a history of extensive involvement with violent entertainment are well documented. Michael Carneal, the fourteen-year-old who fired on a group of classmates at Heath High School in West Paducah, Kentucky, in 1997 was obsessed with violent games—as was the Jonesboro shooter and all the others. Dr. Jim McGee, the FBI consultant who did the FBI "Classroom Avenger" profile of school shooters found that every one of them was immersed in media violence. Phil Chalmers, in his excellent book *Inside the Mind of a Teen Killer*, observed this connection as well. In his extensive interviews and correspondence with a large number of teen killers, Chalmers reports that the one factor every one of them had in common was an obsession with media violence.

It should give us pause to realize that *never* in human history was there a multiple homicide committed by a juvenile against people in his or her own school until 1975. Over the past two decades horrifying crimes by teens under the influence of violent media is growing into a worldwide phenomenon.

Only eight days after the 1999 Columbine High School massacre, fourteen-year-old Todd Cameron Smith walked into his school in Taber, Canada, and randomly shot students, killing one. In Thailand in 2003, seventeen-year-old Anatcha Boonkwan killed two after losing a fistfight with one of his classmates. In 2004 in Carmen, Argentina, a fifteen-year-old student described as a "timid boy who never displayed any violent attitudes" opened fire in his high school, killing four students and injuring five others. The all-time record in human history for a juvenile mass murder (not just in a school, but anywhere) was set in Germany by a seventeen-year-old. On March 11, 2009, Tim

Kretschmer walked into his former high school and started shooting, killing sixteen before taking his own life.

Youth enamored with violent entertainment can become angry young adults, intent on killing. Seung-Hui Cho, the twenty-three-year-old who killed thirty-two people at Virginia Tech University in 2007, was, according to the *Washington Post*, a big fan of violent video games, specifically Counterstrike. Twenty-seven-year-old Steven Kazmierczak who on February 14, 2008, killed five people and injured another twenty-one before committing suicide, spent many childhood hours in a dark room watching horror films. Movie theater gunman James Holmes, who killed twelve people in Aurora, Colorado, on July 20, 2012, and Jared Lee Loughner, who killed six and injured thirteen, including Representative Gabby Giffords, in a 2011 Arizona shooting, were caught up in violent video games as youth.

Violent entertainment continues to train young killers to this day. Since Adam Lanza entered an elementary school, killing twenty-six on December 14, 2012 (as of this writing), there have been forty-four school shootings. Sixty-four percent of the shootings took place at K through 12 schools and thirty-six percent took place on college or university campuses. And another disturbing trend now begins to emerge—young children learning how to kill from violent entertainment. On August 25, 2013, an eight-year-old boy got up from his PlayStation 3, found the family gun, and shot his grandmother in the back of the head, killing her instantly. He had been playing Grand Theft Auto IV.

MEDIA VIOLENCE IS A
SIGNIFICANT FACTOR

You may be thinking, "It's about guns, not video games," right? When we consider the intense brutality of these rampages and cold-blooded murders we have to think carefully about what has changed to cause this. If we only blame increased access to guns we're missing the point, since the availability of guns has been more or less a constant factor in the violence equation in the United States. It is undeniably tragic that our kids have access to weapons. But the question we should be asking is *why kids want to pick up weapons with the intent to kill in the first place.*

Others may want to blame the decay of societal values. While not a good thing for any of us, it's hardly enough of a reason to explain why children are killing in cold blood. If you run down all the possible factors, the myriad explanations, you will eventually come to one thing: the TV, movies, video games, and other media that our kids are spending inordinate amounts of their time with. If you ask what's really changed, that's it. Over the last two decades we have increased the levels of our exposure to graphic violent imagery on our TVs, in our movies, on our home computers, tablets, and handheld devices, and on our gaming consoles. And we have done so under the veil of acceptability, while the violent images gradually grow more realistic and sadistic.

With our kids' screen time at an all-time high, inappropriate violent entertainment saturates their lives. The statistics are sobering. In any given week, children in the

United States between the ages of eight and eighteen spend on average forty hours with screen technologies—not counting the time they are on iPads, laptops, and computers at school. During those forty hours, week after week, kids will see and experience extraordinary amounts of gruesome content since 90 percent of movies and 60 percent of TV shows depict graphic violent imagery. In fact, by age eighteen, a U.S. youth will have seen at least 40,000 simulated murders and 200,000 acts of violence on television alone.

All kids are likely to be affected by cumulative exposure to media violence in some way—some kids will take on a mean attitude; others may become meaner *and* tend to get into fights more often; some will become fearful, others more callous. We will examine these important effects of media violence in more detail in chapter 2. And while the vast majority of young people do not respond to violent media in the extreme ways discussed above, the point is, some do. Media violence plays a part in this. How could it not?

Individually and as a society we need to be taking the influence of violent entertainment much more seriously than we are. Major scientific studies have linked media violence consumption to seriously violent behavior. A seminal 2013 study that appeared in the journal *Youth Violence and Juvenile Justice* presented violent video game exposure as a significant contributor to delinquency, even to psychopathic personality disorders. And in February 2013, the National Science Foundation issued a comprehensive report on youth violence, acknowledging media violence as one of the top three risk factors for violent behavior, right up there with access to guns and mental health.

The degree to which media violence impacts the actions and attitudes of youth will vary widely depending upon critical risk and protective factors—as we shall see later in this chapter. It's never one thing. There are always several factors that come together to cause a young person to kill. But that said, we wrote this book because too many people too readily dismiss the idea that media violence could be such a persuasive influence on some kids.

So the important question is not "Does media violence cause our kids to kill?" The real question is how amid this wide variance of behavioral outcomes we can accurately understand the potentially harmful effects of media violence, especially violent video games, on our kids, so we can find the right solutions.

Or to put it another way: How do we significantly lessen violent entertainment as a contributing factor to training a killer?

CRIME IS "DOWN"—SO WHAT?

A long-standing argument for dismissing media violence as an influencing agent in our kids' lives goes like this: Violent crime, as measured by murders and aggravated assaults, has been declining over the past decade. But media violence, especially the popularity of violent video games over that same decade, has been increasing. Thus, media violence can't be a significant influence on kids' aggression or in their desire to harm others.

This is a flawed argument, however, because it fails to look at the multiple factors that influence the downturn in violent crime. It also fails to put crime statistics in perspective, seeing them as the "evidence" that media violence doesn't contribute to real-life violence. To put youth violence in accurate focus, along with the role of media violence in contributing to it, we need to understand six important points about crime statistics:

1. Advances in Life-Saving Technologies

Murder rates go down when people who are assaulted don't die. The vast progress in medical technology, including everything from mouth-to-mouth resuscitation to the national 911 emergency telephone system to advances in medical technology, has helped us save more lives over the last fifty years, contributing to a downward trend in the murder rate. In 1975, scholar James Q. Wilson has estimated that "if the quality of medical care, especially trauma and emergency care, were the same as it was in 1957, today's murder rate would be three times higher." In 2002, Anthony Harris and a team of researchers from the University of Massachusetts and Harvard University came to similar conclusions. The landmark study in the journal *Homicide Studies* concluded that medical technology advances since 1970 have prevented approximately three out of four murders. That is, if we had 1970s-level medical technology, the murder rate would be three or four times higher than it is today.

2. Criminals Are off the Street

Another factor contributing to a downward trend in violent crime is locking up violent criminals, something that we have been doing at an unprecedented rate. The per capita incarceration rate in the United States more than quadrupled between 1970, when it was at 97 people per 100,000, and 1997, when it reached 440 per 100,000. In 2012 the per capita incarceration rate was 730 people per 100,000, the highest incarceration rate in the world. According to criminologist John J. DiIulio, "dozens of credible empirical analyses . . . leave no doubt that the increased use of prisons averted millions of serious crimes."

3. Aging Population

We also need to consider the positive effects of an aging population. The prime years for violent crime are roughly the years from ages sixteen to twenty-four. As the baby boomers have aged out of the "prime crime" years, the numbers of citizens in their teens and twenties out on the streets has gone down significantly. It makes sense that this would also contribute to bringing down the rate of violent crime.

4. Crime Prevention

Another significant reason for a downturn in violent crime has been more programs for preventing it. In addition, the police technology available to apprehend and convict the violent offender has made steady, significant progress over the years. Portable two-way radios, computerized finger-printing systems and ID checks, DNA matching, video monitoring, security cameras, predictive policing through sophisticated analytics, and other technological innovations have increased the odds of detection, capture, and conviction, and to that extent are acting as a deterrent to crime by helping to incarcerate violent criminals.

5. Underreporting and Inaccurate Records

Crime statistics are general indicators of the level of violence in society, but not a true measure of the level of violence. *The real level of violence will always exceed the level indicated by the crime rates because crimes are not always reported.* According to government surveys, between 2006 and 2010, throughout the United States, 52 percent of violent crimes, 60 percent of property crimes, and 65 percent of rapes and sexual assaults were never reported to the police. Writing in the *New York Times* on the subject, Seth Stephens-Davidowitz points out, "When reported crime drops, it is always possible that this is a result not of a decline in crime itself but of factors that make it more difficult to report crime," such as budget cuts. In his research Stephens-Davidowitz found that "overworked teachers, doctors and nurses may be that much less likely to go through with the reporting process . . . Even primary care doctors, who are legally mandated to report suspected child abuse, admit in surveys that they do not report 27 percent of suspicious incidents." In a seminal article, *Children and Guns: The Hidden Toll*, Michael Luo and Mike McIntire reviewed "hundreds of child firearm deaths" and found that there were far more victims of crime than the records show. Citing "idiosyncrasies" in reporting that vary from state to state they found that "accidental shootings occurred roughly twice as often as the records indicate." And in some cases, when they were reported accidental shootings weren't even defined as crimes.

6. Crime Rates Do Not Equal Number of Crimes Committed

Another important fact to be considered is that violent crime statistics are measures of crime *rates* (generally per 100,000 people), not of the total number of crimes committed, which is determined by both the crime rate and the size of the population. We can easily fail to recognize this distinction because of the way that data is presented. For instance, in his book *The Better Angels of Our Nature: Why Violence Has Declined*, cognitive neuroscientist Steven Pinker makes the case that, over a psychosocial evolutionary span of several thousand years, violence has declined. He marshals evidence to support this hypothesis from a broad range of disciplines. But the title *Why Violence Has Declined* misleads us. It would be more accurate to say: *Why the Rate of Violence Has Declined*. Pinker argues that violence is declining by comparing rates of violent deaths, by war and homicide. For what Pinker is doing this is necessary because he looks at evolutionary trends over thousands of years, and across very diverse populations of people.

However, we need to keep in mind the difference between the rate of violent deaths, and the total number of violent deaths for a given population, so we don't jump to inaccurate conclusions. In the comparisons that Pinker makes, it is possible, even likely, that the rate of violent deaths may be decreasing even as the total number of deaths increases. For instance, in an early, agrarian society of a thousand people, ten people might die violent deaths. In a population of 1 million people, the same rate would be ten thousand deaths. Or, in a population of 1 billion people, the same rate would be 10 million deaths.

Now, if the rate of violent deaths for this larger population is reduced by one-half, that would be "only" 5 million deaths. Are these 5 million deaths somehow preferable to having ten people die in the smaller population because they represent only one-half the death rate of the smaller population? Or, is there something of vital, human concern that is not captured in crime rate or violent death rate statistics?

Crime rates do not focus on trends. Alan Lankford of the University of Alabama analyzed data on random mass murders using an NYPD study of active shooters, counting the incidence of murder attempts in a confined area that resulted in at least two casualties. He found that in the 1980s there were 18 such mass murders, in the 1990s there were 54, and in the 2000s there were 87—a disturbing growth trend that if unheeded will threaten everyone's safety.

The popular argument that violent entertainment has no significant effect because the violent crime rates are down is a nice illusion. But it keeps us complacently defending media violence. In fact, focusing on crime rates keeps us headed in the wrong direction. Better to look where our kids are headed as their lives become increasingly saturated by violence.

VIRTUAL VIOLENCE FUELS
REAL-WORLD VIOLENCE

Children and teens deal with much more violence in their daily lives than crime rates indicate. Figure 1 shows a snapshot of violent behaviors in American schools in the year 2010. The number of deaths at the top of the pyramid propels the renewed search for solutions. And rightly so. But what about the entire pyramid of violence? The layers below the tip demonstrate the alarming amounts of physical and relational aggression going on. Assaults have become commonplace. Every month at least 282,000 students are attacked in our nation's high schools alone, with a staggering total of 3,384,000 physical attacks in all U.S. schools yearly. The base of the pyramid with its 25 million acts of bullying further indicates the nightmare school has become for many kids. Increased aggression brings with it fear and anxiety. Studies show that bullied children are at increased risk for anxiety, depression, substance abuse, and mental disorders. An estimated 160,000 children miss school every day due to fear of attack or intimidation by other students. And when they do come to school more of them are coming armed. One out of every twenty students has seen a student with a gun at school. So, even though a school massacre is remote, schools are far from the safe havens we would like them to be.

If we address the influence of media violence at the

Incidents of Violent Behaviors in American Schools, 2010

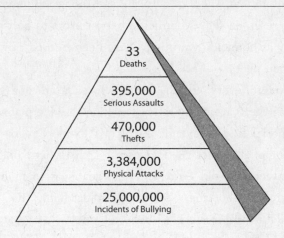

33
Deaths

395,000
Serious Assaults

470,000
Thefts

3,384,000
Physical Attacks

25,000,000
Incidents of Bullying

Sources: www.bullystatistics.org; www.bullyingfacts.info; Bureau of Justice Statistics: Indicators of School Crime and Safety, 2011; National Center for Education Statistics

root, the base of the pyramid, we are likely to see less violent actions by our kids at the ascending layers, even at the tip. If we don't acknowledge and take action on how media violence contributes to increased bullying, then we can expect increases at each level of the pyramid, including more "tip incidents"—massacres of our youth by our youth.

While it's certainly true that mean kids have always been around, there is nothing in our past history to compare with the crisis of cruelty in today's schools: 71 percent of students report bullying as a significant problem, and more than 56 percent have actually witnessed a bullying crime while they were at school, defined as "an intentional act to cause bodily or psychological harm." For some of these victims, especially isolated kids prone to violence, relentless bullying becomes the straw that breaks the camel's back. Feeling desperate and thinking that no one is there to help them, they turn to guns. Among students of all ages, research shows homicide perpetrators to be twice as likely as homicide victims to have been bullied previously by their peers.

And for every bullying victim who succeeds in a revenge killing there are many attempts. Like the one planned for Memorial Day weekend, 2013, in Albany, Oregon. With the help of explosive devices, checklists, and diagrams, seventeen-year-old Gran Acord's "goal was to model the Columbine shootings with some adjustments that would make it a greater success," Benton County district attorney John Haroldson said. The teen hid six types of explosives in a secret floorboard compartment in his bedroom. Authorities also identified notebooks, one of which was called "The (Loosely Stated) 'Plan' AKA Worst Case Scenario," according to news sources compiled by Lauren Hansen in an article she wrote for the online magazine *The Week*. Ms. Hansen explained:

> *The writings indicated that Acord idolized the Columbine shooters and attempted to appropriate their look and weaponry. The teen wrote that the plot would begin after first period, when he would retreat to the parking lot to prepare. At about 11:10 a.m. he would blast music from the car and walk toward the school, napalm firebomb in one hand and a duffel bag in the other. The plan goes on to quote lines from the 2003 movie* Bad Boys II *and explain where he would throw the bombs and when he would kill him-*

self. . . . The county's district attorney said the attack could have happened at any time. "I can't say enough about how lucky we are that there was an intervention," he said. "I shudder to think what could have happened here."

Acord's meticulous plot, detailed with precision, didn't hatch out of thin air. Rather, the myriad influences he encountered as a boy and young teen helped form it. John Dewey, the great educator, was fond of saying, "the environment teaches," meaning that children learn through what surrounds them whether or not we are directly teaching them. Kids absorb values and attitudes—and imitate actions—from what they see and hear. The media environment teaches. And violent entertainment not only influences kids to become meaner but sanctions hostility toward others as well. With the increase in media violence over the decades, our kids' lives have become filled with aggression, anxiety, and despair.

For instance, the popularity of social media has also turned it into a type of teen sport to make others miserable. Why has all this social brutality erupted? While the anonymity of the Internet certainly plays a part, role models from violent media also contribute to molding kids. Kids don't wake up one day and decide to harm others. Hostile attitudes and behaviors take time to ripen. And a steady diet of media violence helps develop them.

If we had a stranger living in our homes teaching our kids how to fire headshots with precision or if we encountered a teacher in the school training kids to communicate with others so they would want to harm themselves, we wouldn't allow it. We would put a stop to it at once. By not explicitly addressing the influence of media violence in our kids' daily lives, we give it implicit permission to do such teaching and training.

Consider that over half of adolescents have been bullied online, and about the same number have engaged in cyberbullying. When the first edition of this book was released fifteen years ago, few teens were engaging in cyberbullying—in fact, so few that many people would ask us, "What's cyberbullying?" They needed it explained in more detail because they had never heard of it! Today, cyberbullying is no longer an unknown word but a real crisis causing extreme stress. The typical teen taunts of the past have morphed into serious threats such as "If you come to school tomorrow, I will kill you." How can kids cope with such a constant dark presence in their lives? The sad fact is that many of them can't.

Twelve-year-old Rebecca Ann Sedwick received relentless online messages from fifteen middle school girls like "Can U die please?" The school, despite an antibullying policy, couldn't stop these. So her mother placed Rebecca in a new school and shut down her Facebook page, while keeping tabs on her social-media footprint. But, unknown to her mother, Rebecca had downloaded new applications on her cell phone—ask.fm, Kik, and Voxer—making it possible for Rebecca to continue to receive the hostile text messages. Rebecca didn't tell her mom about these. In retrospect, her mom thinks Rebecca hid that information because she feared that if she did reveal it, her mom would

Media Violence Influences Both Bullies and Victims

Media Violence

- Increases Aggression
- Develops a Perceived Right to Bully

Much of
Media Violence Models
Dominator/Victim
Relationships

- Increases Fear
- Develops Anxiety and/or Sense of Helplessness

Bully ◀——————▶ Victim

Dominator/Victim
Relationships
Acted Out in Real World

take away her cell phone. So rather than confiding in her mother, Rebecca silently endured, until she couldn't take it anymore. She changed one of her online screen names to "That Dead Girl" and messaged a friend: "I'm jumping." Then Rebecca went to an abandoned concrete plant, climbed a tower, and leapt to her death.

According to a 2008 study from the Yale School of Medicine's Child Study Center, Rebecca is not alone in her desperation. Cyberbullying victims consider suicide more often than nonvictims. In fact, there is a strong connection between bullying, being bullied, and suicide. Sadly, suicide is the third leading cause of death for youth, ages ten to twenty-four, after accidents and homicide.

And, tragically, suicide rates among adolescents have grown more than 50 percent in the past thirty years.

The dominator/victim relationship, often graphically sadistic, has become more commonplace in films and video games. While they may be rated R or M for adults, that doesn't keep some children and teens from seeing them. For example, a 2008 study of 6,500 children ages ten through fourteen, conducted by Dr. Keliah A. Worth of Dartmouth Medical Center found that the movie *Gangs of New York* was seen by children as young as ten years old. In the film the character played by Daniel Day-Lewis lays out Leonardo DiCaprio's character on a table, beats him with his fists and head, and finally brands his face with a hot knife blade to permanently scar and humiliate him. One of the incidents in Grand Theft Auto IV, played by children as young as eight years old, is killing a woman and jumping up and down on her while blood gushes forth from her body.

The dominator/victim roles are acted out in depictions of relational aggression as well. The reality TV show *The Apprentice*, popular with teens, contains eighty-five acts of verbal or relational aggression per hour. Even young children's programs aren't immune from insults and put-downs. In an analysis of children's programming by Dr. Cynthia Scheibe, it was found that the average children's show contained insults 96 percent of the time.

It's not just that the media violence models aggressive behavior as an acceptable form of self-expression, especially for kids already prone to aggression. Media violence also gives an implicit sanction to the *form* of the dominator/victim relationship. It tells our kids that one person (the bully) gets to do whatever he or she wants (and can get away with) to another person (the victim). And that person (the victim) "gets" to experience whatever the bully chooses to do. In fact, the bully chooses the experience for both parties. The victim, on the other hand, is not allowed any choice, except how he or she will suffer.

Bullies seldom act alone. In fact, part of being a bully is acceptance by a peer group. Bullies gather power in numbers. Victims, on the other hand, are usually outnumbered and socially isolated. Victims live in a pressure cooker of hate. As the pressure of the bullying builds up, day after day, and the suffering becomes more intense, the victim is faced with two basic options. The first is to get adult help to escape or stop the bullying. If this is not possible, the second option is to find ways to endure the bullying.

If the victim cannot escape, stop, or endure the bullying, then the pressure continues to build beyond his or her capacity to cope. One pathway a victim might take to relieve the intolerable pressure is through explosion, and we witness a rampage shooting. The other pathway out is through implosion, and we get to attend the funeral of a young person who committed suicide.

Because the portrayal of dominator/victim relationships is so pervasive in media violence, and because media play such a massive role in the lives of children and youth, there is an implicit social sanction normalizing the violence of the dominator/victim relationship. As children grow into the dominator role, acting it out in peer groups, practicing it over and over with violent video games, bullying others starts to feel normal. There is a sense of rightness to the domination, a sense of "I have the right to treat others this way." And the victim feels this implicit social sanction as disempowerment. This is one important reason it is so difficult, even with adult help, for the victim to escape the pressure cooker—because the form of the relationship appears to be "normal." Thanks to media violence portrayals, it can seem to youth that society is saying it's okay to bully and to be a victim—that it is normal for a dominator/victim relationship to exist.

Parents, teachers, and authorities, individually and together, work hard to protect kids from the forest fire of bullying sweeping our country. And while a few victories are won from time to time, bullying continues to increase. All of the efforts to stop bullying are like trying to put out a fire while someone goes around and dumps gasoline on the hot spots. Media violence is that gasoline. Until we recognize and address its influence on bullying through the modeling and sanctioning of the dominator/victim relationship, it is unlikely that we will succeed in putting out the fire of bullying that rages in our schools today.

WE EITHER PROTECT KIDS
OR WE PUT THEM AT RISK

The 2001 U.S. Surgeon General's report on youth violence stated that "the bulk of research that has been done on risk factors identifies and measures their predictive value separately, without taking into account the influence of other risk factors. More important than any individual factor, however, is the accumulation of risk factors." Media violence is one of those risk factors in shaping youth to become violent. When you add other risk factors to the equation, you increase the chances of murderous rages. John Zawahri, for instance, was repeatedly beaten by an abusive father and saw his mother beaten as well. This obviously made him angry and depressed. The violent video games he played gave him ideas and permission for his decision to go on a killing spree. The impact of media violence always interacts with the other risk factors. Decades of research have identified the main risk factors contributing to violent behavior:

- An abusive home life and/or unstable family situation
- Poverty
- Media violence
- Anger and depression
- Pornography
- Cults and gangs; pressure to join a gang
- Easy access to and fascination with weapons
- Peer pressure
- Introduction to a criminal lifestyle by a family member or friend
- Bullying
- Drug and alcohol abuse
- Lack of spiritual guidance and appropriate discipline
- Mental illness and brain injuries

The more risk factors children experience, the more likely it is that serious violence will erupt at moments of severe stress. It is precisely at such moments that kids are most likely to revert to their earliest, most visceral remembrance of violence. Consider the power of such violent "imprinting" on a little boy who watches his dad beat his mom repeatedly. He is two, three, four, or five years old and he despises this behavior and hates his father. But if he is not careful, twenty years later, when he is under stress and he has a wife and kids, what is he likely to do? He will do the same thing he saw his father do. Why? He, of all people, should understand how despicable this behavior is, how much his children will hate him. How much he'll hate himself. But he can't help it—it was burned into his system at an early age and imprinted on how he deals with like situations.

Now imagine that this little boy not only observes domestic violence but is also physically abused himself. He distracts himself from the pain he experiences by watching television. Like 65 percent of kids in our country, he escapes to his bedroom and watches TV or downloads movies. He likes watching violence. The violent imagery, in fact, reinforces and justifies the violence he is experiencing in the home. How much more likely is it that he will become a violent abuser himself?

An estimated 4 million American children are victimized each year through physical abuse, sexual abuse, domestic violence, community violence, and other traumatic events. When television is added to this equation, more stress is added to the child's life. Research has found that abused children watch more television than other children do, prefer violent programs, and appear to admire violent heroes. Children who are both abused and watchers of a great deal of television are more likely to commit violent crimes later in life.

Along with risk factors, there are protective ones too, thankfully. The cumulative risk of violent behavior lessens with more protective factors in the child's life. Important protective factors include the following:

- A stable family life with loving, involved parents
- Good school performance, enjoyment of learning and reading
- Development of talents outside screen technologies, such as music, dance, art, and sports; studying a foreign language
- A mutually supportive peer group
- Active involvement in a religion and/or spiritual guidance
- Community participation
- Involvement in school activities such as student council or the debate team
- Media literacy education in schools
- No TV or screen time from birth through age two, and one hour or less per day with all forms of screen technology throughout childhood
- Rules and consistent enforcement for both content viewed and use of media and digital devices, such as a bedroom free of TV and keeping the TV off when no one is watching it throughout childhood and adolescence
- Specific, purposeful use of all screen technologies— little or no multitasking with many forms of screen technology, such as being on the computer doing homework while playing video games, texting, and using social media
- Regular family conversations and family meetings to discuss potentially contentious issues before they erupt
- Frequent conversations about violent media and media in general with parents and caring adults

- Preventive measures, such as counseling, before anger or depression get out of hand
- Stress reduction and meditation techniques
- Healthy lifestyle habits of physical activity and good nutrition

Protective factors, even when alongside some risk factors, can ameliorate the harmful effects of media violence. For instance, a single mother who lives in poverty in a gang-infested neighborhood has significant challenges to overcome. But by being caringly involved in her children's lives, such as making sure she talks to them often and reads to them when they are young, she puts them on a positive trajectory mentally and emotionally, imparting skills for resisting a gang lifestyle. If she nurtures and encourages academic achievement and development of their innate talents, she gives them great gifts in helping them to maximize their potential as they mature, increasing their chances for escaping poverty and gangs as well. Her children develop reading and study habits, along with clear priorities for personal success and fulfillment. If she decides additionally to keep their bedroom TV free throughout their childhood and adolescence, and she talks frequently with them about media violence, she keeps the doors open for important communication that allows her to understand how they may be perceiving and processing the violent images they do see, and she can intervene with teachable moments as needed. So, by attending to many of those "little things" that parents can do in daily living routines, this mother can put significant protective factors in place that can positively counteract the risk factors in her children's lives.

Realistically, then, any given child or teen, on any given day, has a mix of both risk and protective factors. Both types of factors interact continually in children's lives, determining how media violence will influence behaviors and attitudes. When we think about how many of our kids spend their days immersed in screen violence while dealing daily with physical and relational aggression, it should give us pause to consider just how much our kids are up against. And take a look at those risk factors again. The majority of them are mirrored in our kids' favorite screen entertainment. Repetitive media images depicting the protective factors, on the other hand, are not as easily found.

Unfortunately, graphic, horrific violent entertainment probably won't go away soon.

So let's make conscious efforts to increase the protective factors and decrease the risk factors. In doing so, we "immunize" kids against the potentially harmful effects of media violence, lessening the likelihood of more massacres in the process.

CHAPTER TWO

THE COMPELLING
EVIDENCE

One ship you can ignore, but not an armada.

—Adrian Raine, *The Anatomy of Violence*

The debate should be over by now. And for many of us, it is. Scientific evidence overwhelmingly supports media violence as a significant factor contributing to increased aggression and fear, desensitization to human suffering, and the need for increased levels of violence to feel fulfilled. In fact, in 2000, based on decades of conclusive evidence, six prestigious organizations that focus on public health issues—the American Psychological Association, the American Academy of Pediatrics, the American Academy of Family Physicians, the American Psychiatric Association, the American Medical Association, and the American Academy of Child and Adolescent Psychiatry—issued a joint statement that, in part, reads, "At this time, well over

1,000 studies . . . point overwhelmingly to a causal connection between media violence and aggressive behavior in some children."

Yes, doctors, psychologists, and psychiatrists really did say the word "causal." At a Senate Commerce Committee hearing on neurobiological research and the impact of media on children, Dr. Michael Rich, director of the Center on Media and Children's Health at the Children's Hospital of Boston, testified to Congress in 2003 that the correlation between violent media and aggressive behavior "is stronger than that of calcium intake and bone mass, lead ingestion and lower IQ, condom non-use and sexually acquired HIV, and environmental tobacco smoke and lung cancer, all associations that clinicians accept as fact, and on which preventive medicine is based without question." Jeffrey McIntyre, legislative and federal affairs officer for the American Psychological Association, puts it succinctly: "To argue against the correlation between violent entertainment and aggression is like arguing against gravity."

But note, in the joint statement the experts make the causal relationship even clearer by saying three important words, "in some children." We understand smoking contributes to lung cancer, but not all people who smoke will suffer from lung cancer. If we add in a genetic predisposition—a mother or father dying from a lung cancer, for instance—along with growing up in a smoke-filled environment, we increase the odds that our smoking will play an increased role in our getting lung cancer. That's why our primary care physician noses around in our daily business. Our habits will let her know if we are at risk. And if we are, our doctor in her integrity and within her professional code of ethics must go over the preventive measures with us. She will lay out in detail how we need to change our lifestyle in order to reduce our risk of dying from lung cancer. And if we're smart, we'll listen to her.

As a society we accept the science of health risks, yet still remain steadfastly in denial about the relationship between media violence and increased aggression. It seems the television, movie, and video game industries have a hold on us like the tobacco industry did several decades ago. We would rather be fooled by a billion-dollar force that keeps getting richer from our kids' violent entertainment habits than logically accept the facts as we do now for lung cancer. People once dismissed the scientific evidence demonstrating smoking to be a dangerous habit; we are now in a similar position regarding media violence. Tobacco advertisers targeted youth. More children recognized Joe Camel than they did popular cartoons at the time. And as ludicrous as it may sound, denial ran so deep that even some physicians back then were saying it was okay to smoke. The parallels with media violence today are uncanny. The media industry markets directly to youth—violent video games are cool. And many well-educated people still don't believe the connection between media violence and increased aggression exists. Contrary to popular belief, our brains aren't as logical as we think. Logic indicates that with more information, more hard-data evidence, we would change our beliefs. Make sense? One would think. But not so simple. As Leonard Mlodinow observes in his book *Subliminal: How Your Unconscious Mind Rules Your Behavior*, "The 'causal

The "Causal Arrow"

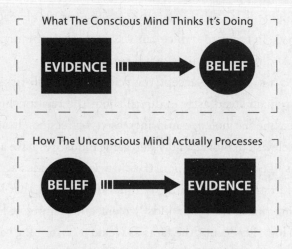

Source: Adapted from *Subliminal: How Your Unconscious Mind Rules Your Behavior* by Leonard Mlodinow.

arrow' in human thought processes consistently tends to point from belief to evidence, not viceversa."

Mlodinow cites studies showing that we more readily accept evidence that supports what we want to believe. He tells us, "Psychologists call this 'motivated reasoning' and explains that it "shapes the way we understand and interpret our environment, especially our social environment, and it helps us justify our preferred beliefs. . . . Our unconscious can choose from an entire smorgasbord of interpretations to feed our conscious mind. In the end we feel we are chewing on the facts, though we've actually been chomping on a preferred conclusion."

Human brains process a lot of stuff unconsciously and

we form beliefs largely unconsciously. New information entering into conscious awareness can rattle us, creating cognitive dissonance. What we "know" to be true may very well not be. Disoriented and disturbed, we usually feel the need to do something about the situation—to resolve the dissonance. We may do something easy like quickly dismissing the evidence or something more difficult like letting go of cherished beliefs and allowing in the new ideas. The latter often takes time and a lot of careful thought, requiring an open, inquisitive mind. Closed minds don't do so well at accepting ideas that conflict with established beliefs.

Based on observation, a parent may conclude, "My child watches violent cartoons and he is fine." Is she seeing only what she wants to see? Perhaps. Screenwriters and video game developers—anyone who has a vested interest in the issue—could have a difficult time acknowledging that what they have created or dispersed is potentially harmful to kids. Do they secretly feel guilty and want to justify their actions? We may never know and, interestingly, neither may they. That's the inherent nature of unconscious processes.

The current crisis, with children's and teens' lives so steeped in real and screen violence, should cause us to open our minds a little bit and work to gain greater self-awareness. Denial will keep us chained to inaction and unproductive, repetitive debates, ultimately dooming our kids to increased vulnerability to the negative influences of violent entertainment.

So, as you read the scientific research in this chapter, remember, you don't have to believe it for it to be true.

THE PATTERN OF DENIAL AND
DEBATE, DEBATE AND DENIAL

B efore we get to the key findings of the seminal scientific research on media violence, a look at the insidious
pattern we've been stuck in over the last sixty years may
be enlightening. The pattern goes like this:

Violent content is created and shown on TV and in movies and, more recently, video games. This violent imagery
has to become increasingly sensational and horrific to capture attention, resulting in the dismal state we are in today
with violent content almost beyond human imagination in
many circumstances. Children and teens watch this violent
imagery and play violent video games. Some of them act out
in real life the violence they see on the screen; others do not.
Scientists and academics research why this is so. They share
their findings in academic journals, at professional conferences, and, if they are lucky, in a radio or TV interview.

Government authorities like the surgeon general make
firm recommendations based on what the researchers and
experts are saying. The industry that creates the violent
content, whether it's the TV, movie, or video game industry, addresses the concerns in ways that will keep their
violent content available but within protective boundaries,
such as ratings systems. This provides a "choice" for parents. Parents, frustrated and confused, must continually
deal with "choices" that become more constrained in the
media industry's favor.

And then, as too few parents and professionals are
accurately informed about this crucial information, mass

media spins the question as a distracting debate, while violent imagery in television, movies, and video games gets more sensational and horrifying and our kids become increasingly affected and infected by it. And nothing significant happens that prevents the ever-growing media violence technology tsunami from engulfing the hearts and minds of our kids.

That's been the pattern since 1954—with similar sneaky tactics the tobacco industry used so successfully for so long.

Sixty Years of Denial and Debate

The pattern of denial and debate started with television violence, then spread to movie and, now video game violence. It's true that graphic violence in books, comic books, and music can also affect children and teens negatively. However, in keeping with the goals of this book, we focus on TV and video game violence in describing the sixty-year history below of expert recommendations, controversy, policy recommendations, and stymied actions.

The 1950s

The possibility that television increases aggression has been raised virtually since the advent of TV viewing in America. The first U.S. congressional hearings on the question took place in 1952, when only around a quarter of American households had television sets and when what was on TV was, by current standards, fairly slow and boring. The U.S. Senate hearings on television violence held before the Senate Subcommittee on Juvenile Delinquency discussed whether television violence was contributing to real-life violence in the United States. These procedures began the model of expert testimony on TV violence in front of Congress that is still in place today. Many highly regarded experts testified that since the risk was so great and the payoff so small, television violence was a totally unacceptable risk. However, network executives claimed that the available research was not conclusive.

The 1960s

In 1961, Newton Minow, then the newly appointed chairman of the FCC, sat down and watched one full week of television in preparation for his inaugural address to the National Association of Broadcasters (NAB). Minow's advice to the broadcasters of the 1960s could be addressed to those of today (except that today our "stations" never go off the air):

> I invite you to sit down in front of your television set when your station goes on the air and stay there . . . until the station signs off. I can assure you that you will observe a vast wasteland. You will see a procession of game shows, violence, audience participation shows, formula comedies about totally unbelievable families, blood and thunder, mayhem, violence, sadism, murder, western bad men, western good men, private eyes, gangsters, more violence and cartoons.

Although broadcasters responded to Minow's speech by

agreeing to assign large parts of the UHF spectrum to public broadcasting, they did not take violent programming off the air, nor reduce violent content. But the "vast wasteland" remained a metaphor for television content throughout the 1970s.

In 1969, Senator John Pastore from Rhode Island, chair of the Senate Subcommittee on Communications, held a hearing to which he invited the usual group of parents, teachers, social scientists, and network executives. He also invited the surgeon general of the United States, something that had never been done before. The surgeon general had just concluded the first report on smoking and health, which caused quite a stir because it indicated a link between smoking and lung cancer, a very difficult relationship to accept at the time. When the surgeon general subsequently commented on TV violence, he put the issue in the same context as the smoking controversy—as a public health issue. That said a lot.

The 1970s

The surgeon general's report, *Television and Growing Up: The Impact of Televised Violence*, was released in 1972 and stated that there was strong evidence that TV violence can be harmful to young viewers. Confirming the accumulating body of research, this three-year study consisting of sixty new research projects further documented that exposure to screen violence increases the likelihood of aggression.

In 1972, the U.S. Surgeon General issued a warning about violent TV programs: "It is clear to me that the causal relationship between televised violence and antisocial behavior is sufficient to warrant appropriate and immediate remedial action. . . . There comes a time when the data are sufficient to justify action. That time has come."

Yet, television networks were simply unwilling to keep a consistent stream of nonviolent programming available to the public. They refused to acknowledge the validity of the compelling body of research consisting of hundreds of studies. As network executives manufactured more and more horror for increased profits, they continued to ignore an unquestionable fact: It was our children who were paying the price. And, of course, they knew that.

The 1980s

In 1981, the newly appointed chair of the FCC, Mark Fowler, prepared for his inaugural address to the NAB in the same way Newton Minow had in 1961—by watching a week of television. However, Fowler came to the opposite conclusion. Instead of a vast wasteland, he saw a "vast richness," despite the fact that TV violence had increased significantly since 1961.

Fowler said that television was just another appliance, "a toaster with pictures," and that we need not be concerned. Yet, in the 1980–81 season, when the FCC was discussing deregulation of children's programming, violence on children's television shows reached its highest level in twenty years: thirty-three acts of violence per hour.

But by 1981, the rate of real-life violence had risen to the level where it was *finally* being identified as a public health issue. Dr. Brandon Centerwall had a lot to do with this. Dr. Centerwall, an epidemiologist, was asked to help start the violence research program at the national Centers for Disease Control in Atlanta, Georgia. A central issue confronting the research team was the doubling of the murder rate in the United States since the 1950s. That the rate had doubled was indisputable. The question was, why?

Dr. Centerwall approached this as a question of epidemiology, searching through rigorous statistical analysis for the causes of the "epidemic of violence." He considered every factor that any research evidence had ever suggested might reasonably be a cause, including changes in urbanization and economic conditions; the effect of the post–World War II baby boom; trends in alcohol abuse, capital punishment, and civil unrest; changes in the availability of firearms; and television. Television was included as part of the array. It was not considered more likely to provide an explanation than any of the other proposed candidates.

After seven years of research that included rigorous testing for confounding cross-relationships with other possible causes, the conclusion was inescapable: "If television technology had never been developed, today there would be 10,000 fewer murders each year in the United States, 70,000 fewer rapes, and 700,000 fewer injurious assaults." The *Journal of the American Medical Association* published Dr. Centerwall's results in 1992. If the study had told us that 10,000 people per year were dying from an infectious disease, it would have made the evening news headlines. Alas, almost nobody in this country has heard of Dr. Centerwall or his findings.

The eighties saw another pivotal report issued by the

National Institute of Mental Health in 1982. This was a review of over 2,500 studies on the effects of TV violence—about fourteen volumes of documentation. The conclusion indicated a consensus among members of the research community that "in magnitude, television violence is as strongly correlated with aggressive behavior as any other behavioral variable that has been measured."

The television industry didn't respond, however, to this very important new data. Instead, deregulation came in 1984, and with it more reason for concern. Now, for the first time ever, toy manufacturers could sponsor or develop cartoons that were no more than "commercials" for their products. By 1987, sales of violent toys had soared more than 600 percent from the 1970s. Cartoons, more violent than ever (in the 60s and 70s), flooded the market, along with their icon toy counterparts with which youngsters could practice violent play when they weren't watching.

The 1990s

Congressional hearings in the late 1980s resulted in the Television Violence Act (TVA) of 1990. This legislation provided the television industry with temporary antitrust immunity so that they could work together to develop "voluntary guidelines" on television violence. The guidelines resulted in the Children's Television Act (CTA), which included the following two provisions:

1. Commercials during children's programs could not exceed 10.5 minutes per hour on weekends and 12 minutes per hour on weekdays.

2. Television broadcast licenses could not be renewed unless the station had complied with the first provision and had served the "educational and information needs of children" by providing at least three hours a week of educational programming.

The Children's Television Act was a joke. In the coming years, many experts and parents would decry the lists of programs that networks identified as "educational." The networks deemed such programs as *G.I. Joe*, *Leave It to Beaver*, *The Jetsons*, and *James Bond, Jr.* as examples of shows that served the educational and informational needs of children.

Between 1996 and 1998, the three-year National Television Violence Study (NTVS) offered a comprehensive evaluation of television violence. Unlike past studies, this project did not merely count the number of violent acts and report them. Rather, the researchers developed nine contextual features to measure the harmful effects of that violence. For instance, they determined that television violence poses the greatest risk if there are repeated acts using a conventional weapon, if violence is put into a humorous context, or if it is morally justified in some way.

The conclusion of the first year of the study was that "psychologically harmful" violence is pervasive on broadcast and cable TV programs. The study found not only that 57 percent of programs contained some violence, but also that the context in which this violence occurred could have harmful effects.

The second- and third-year summaries told similar

stories. TV violence was at an all-time high, with nearly 40 percent of the violent incidents on television initiated by characters who possessed qualities that made them attractive role models. The study also found that youngsters who watched two hours of cartoons each day were exposed to five hundred high-risk portrayals of violence per year that taught aggressive behaviors. And a surprise finding—TV ratings attracted children to violent programs by alerting kids to their existence!

In 1998, the seminal work Children and Media Violence: A Yearbook from the International Clearinghouse on Children and Violence on the Screen was released by UNESCO. This was a four-hundred-page book describing studies of media violence worldwide, including the largest study ever conducted, which surveyed five thousand twelve-year-olds in twenty-three countries, and it thoroughly and irrevocably supported what studies for the last four decades had been claiming—media violence played an important part in increasing aggression.

1990s: Video Game Violence Increases

Yet, despite all the research on the harmful effects of media violence, the video game industry escalated levels of violence with the advent of "first-person shooter video games." In 1992, Wolfenstein 3D made the victims actually bleed, unlike previous games, where victims who were shot disappeared. One year later the extremely popular Doom took "blood and gore" to a new level, allowing players to hunt and kill each other, rather than attacking monsters and demons. Other games soon followed that kept pushing the boundaries of acceptability. For instance, in the Duke Nukem series, the "shooter," Duke, who is controlled by the player and looks somewhat like the Terminator, moves through pornography shops, where he finds posters of scantily clad women he can use for target practice. At advanced levels, bonus points are awarded for the murder of female prostitutes, women who are usually naked. Duke often encounters defenseless, bound women, some of whom are even conveniently tied to columns and plead, "Kill me, kill me." A game called Postal took the horror one step further. The user went "postal" and received points for killing as many innocent victims as possible while they begged for mercy. In the game Redneck Rampage, kids did the same with farm animals and farmers. In House of the Dead, you blew away chunks of the bodies you fired at and got clean kills only for headshots.

The toy industry, as it did with cartoons in the eighties, created action figures to go along with violent games. And these were clearly not for teens. Mortal Kombat action toys were labeled "For children four and up." Duke Nukem action figures became popular with boys as young as eight years old. In fact, Duke Nukem, a video game rated M for mature audiences seventeen and older, was sold in toy stores, shelved next to Eggs of Steel, a kiddie game about an animated egg.

The Entertainment Software Rating Board (ESRB) established in 1994 by the Entertainment Software Association developed ratings for video games, but unfortunately they were not strictly enforced. Many parents didn't even know about them. And if they did, they didn't use them.

A 2004 article in the *Journal of Adolescence* reported that 90 percent of teens in grades 8–12 said that their parents never checked the ratings of video games before allowing a purchase, and fewer than one in five parents had ever kept them from getting a game based on its rating.

The 2000s

In 2000 the tragedy at Columbine High School prompted the joint statement by six professional organizations (who don't have a vested interest in marketing violence, but *do* have a vested interest in the health of children) quoted near the beginning of this chapter.

While experts voiced their concerns, 2001 and 2002 saw several media-related violent acts by youth, including the following: A twelve-year-old Florida boy brutally killed a six-year-old girl by imitating professional wrestling moves. A Texas seventeen-year-old set himself on fire while being videotaped, attempting to imitate the "human barbecue" stunt from the MTV show *Jackass*. Four teens, ages thirteen through seventeen, watched the movie *Menace II Society*, then committed a carjacking and shot two other youths, paralleling the film.

Despite the upsurge in real-world violent acts such as these, levels of violence increased on television as well as in video games. The Parents Television Council, a nonprofit, nonpartisan watchdog group, initiated a three-year study of television content on all the major stations, analyzing a total of four hundred hours of programming. The study found that overall, violence increased in every time slot between 1998 and 2002. On all the networks combined, violence was 41 percent more frequent during the 8:00 p.m. "family hour" in 2002 than in 1998. In 1998, for instance, 29 percent of all violent sequences included the use of guns or other weapons. By 2002, that number increased to 38 percent.

Since 2002 our kids' "entertainment" has become darker and more despairing on all fronts. Today we have amassed enough scientific evidence for the nation's doctors, counselors, social workers, teachers, early childhood educators, pediatricians, psychiatrists, and community health workers to all agree that media violence is a significant factor damaging children's and teens' emotional and social development. Yet, President Obama introduced S. 134, the Violent Content Research Act of 2013 to Congress on January 24, 2013, after the controversy over the role of violent video games in the Newtown massacre. The bill "arranges for the National Academy of Science to study whether there is a connection between violent media exposure and harmful effects on children," including "whether the exposure . . . causes children to act aggressively or causes measurable harm to children." "We don't benefit from ignorance," said Obama.

Now there is nothing wrong with ongoing research regarding the effects of media violence. But the question to ask is not whether there is a connection between media violence and harmful effects on children. We have been asking that for sixty years and we do have the answer to it—a resounding "Yes." The new questions to be asking have to do with how and under what circumstances media violence affects kids. It's no longer a question of if, but of how.

THE FOUR EFFECTS OF
MEDIA VIOLENCE

In the thousands of scientific studies over the last six decades, researchers have documented four basic negative effects from exposure to screen violence: increased aggression, increased fear, desensitization to real-life and screen violence, and increased appetite for more violence—on and off screen. All kids who are exposed to a steady diet of media violence are likely to be affected. As Douglas Gentile, PhD, media violence researcher at Iowa State University, aptly puts it, "that everyone is not affected in the same way does not mean that everyone is not affected."

Let's look at significant research studies for each of the four effects:

1. Increased Aggression

Scientific evidence repeatedly shows that we see more physical violence by children and teens who watch screen violence and/or play violent video games. It's that simple. A 2008 meta-analysis of twenty-six studies involving 13,661 participants found that violent media exposure is significantly linked to violent behavior such as punching, beating, and choking others. And continual exposure, of course, has more long-lasting effects than short-term episodes.

Together with his colleagues, Dr. Craig Anderson, Distinguished Professor and Director of the Center for the Study of Violence at Iowa State University, led a team of researchers who compiled a major summary of the short- and long-term effects of media violence in 2003 that concluded: "Research on violent television films, and video games . . . reveals unequivocal evidence that media violence increases the likelihood of aggressive and violent behavior in both immediate and long-term contexts." Similarly, a comprehensive meta-analysis of violent video games conducted in 2010, which included 381 effects from studies involving 130,295 participants from all over the world, found that violent video games increased aggressive thoughts, angry feelings, physiological arousal, and aggressive behavior. There are three basic reasons that many researchers believe violent video games have strong effects on aggression—stronger even than violent television programs. First, video game playing is an active process, while TV viewing is passive. Second, since players actually participate more in the violence with video game playing, they are more likely to identify with the perpetrators of violence. And third, violent video games reward violent behavior. All the studies in this comprehensive meta-analysis show that when children play mature-rated games, it is more likely that they will be aggressive in real-world situations.

The earlier a child is exposed to any type of media violence, the more likely it is that the increase in aggressive behavior will show up in adulthood. The findings of a major twenty-two-year longitudinal study, between 1963 and 1985 by Professors Leonard Eron and L. Rowell Huesmann, brought this critical "early childhood sensitive period" to light. The researchers followed the fates of 875 children living in a semirural U.S. county. Their findings showed that exposure to TV violence before the age of eight was predictive of aggressive behavior at age nineteen.

Since the study took place over two decades, second-generation effects could be observed: Alarmingly, childhood TV habits predicted criminal arrests at age thirty. Girls and boys watching more television at age eight were later, as mothers and fathers, likely to use physical punishment with their own children more severely than those parents who had watched less television as children. Remarkably, how much television violence a thirty-year-old parent had been watching at age eight predicted his or her children's degree of physical aggressiveness even better than it predicted the parent's own physical aggressiveness at age thirty. The researchers pointed out that aggressive habits learned early in life can be resistant to change and "predictive of serious adult antisocial behavior." Sobering.

In a 1986 study, Eron and Huesmann followed one thousand children from the United States, Australia, Finland, Israel, the Netherlands, and Poland over a three-year period and found that "early viewing of TV violence was significantly associated with higher levels of subsequent aggressive behavior, even after controlling for a child's initial level of aggression." After decades of studying the issue, today Huesmann asserts that the relationship between TV violence and aggression is most likely reciprocal: "Early viewing of violence stimulates aggression, and behaving aggressively then leads to a heightened interest in violent TV content." Some vicious cycle, huh?

Interestingly enough, the more kids watch television, the more aggressive they become—even if the content is nonviolent. But every parent knows this, right? Don't try to take a child on errands after he's been watching television for a few hours. We're all too familiar with what usually happens—a cranky, whining youngster fidgets in the cart or, worse, won't sit still and runs through the aisles, blowing off steam. The need for physical release after sitting for a few hours becomes apparent. Sometimes this physical release leads to lashing out at others. Three important studies help us shed light on this phenomenon.

The Notel Studies

Ever wonder what life could be like without any television? And how life would change once you got it, if you had been accustomed to living without it? In the 1980s, Dr. Tannis McBeth Williams and her associates at the University of British Columbia found out. They investigated the effect of the introduction of television upon the children in a remote rural community, called Notel, for "No Television."

Researchers studied both children and adults before television was introduced into Notel and two years after its introduction. Surprisingly, both the children and adults showed a significant increase in physical and verbal aggression after the two years. Also, children as well as adults more often used aggressive behavior as a successful and acceptable method for achieving goals. The researchers attributed this in part to modeling the violence they did see on television, and also to the fact that lack of physical activity can increase stress levels, making us more prone to be on edge, geared for a fight.

Not too surprisingly, children under eight changed more significantly than older kids or adults. What was surprising, though, was the big jump in aggression. By two years after the introduction of television, rates of physical aggression among Notel's young children had increased by 160 percent! The increase was observed in both boys and girls—in those who were aggressive to begin with and in those who were not.

The Stanford Study

In 2001, a study by Thomas Robinson, MD, and his colleagues at the Department of Pediatrics and Center for Research in Disease Prevention at the Stanford University School of Medicine found that reducing time with TV, movies, and video games also reduced aggressive behaviors on the playground by third and fourth graders, who engaged in about half as many verbally aggressive behaviors—such as teasing, threatening, or taunting their peers—than students at a control school.

And the great news was that the most aggressive students experienced the greatest drop in combativeness. The study concluded, "These findings support the causal influences of these media on aggression and the potential benefits of reducing children's media use." Dr. Robinson added, "Kids spend more time watching television than doing any other thing besides sleeping. It's not unreasonable to expect that this [reducing exposure] will translate into large impacts on their health and behavior over time."

A Seventeen-Year Longitudinal Study

This important longitudinal study, released in 2002 by Jeffrey Johnson, PhD, of Columbia University and his colleagues, tracked a random sample of 707 children in New York state. Results showed that watching seven or more hours of TV during adolescence was associated with an increase in the likelihood of becoming aggressive toward others later in life. This is a hopeful sign. A longitudinal study gives solid evidence for a doable prevention strategy with strong potential—limit TV viewing during early adolescence and in turn reduce the likelihood of aggressive behaviors.

2. Increased Fear

Violent and/or scary TV programs and movies have both immediate and long-term effects on kids, especially young children. Immediate reactions include intense fear, crying, clinging behaviors, and stomachaches. Long-term reactions vary from nightmares and difficulty sleeping to concern about being hurt or killed and aversion to common animals. Cases have been reported of children suffering posttraumatic stress syndrome after watching horror films such as *The Exorcist* and *Invasion of the Body Snatchers*, with hospitalization being required in some cases. A persistent diet of fear-inducing movies, TV programs, and video games can have deleterious effects on children's brains. Dr. Bruce Perry, director of the Child Trauma Center at Baylor University, has found that exposure to chronic stress results in functional deficits in children's brains and increased vulnerability to future stressors.

Scary images are so stressful for youngsters because they do not interpret images like adults do. When television networks replayed the image of the planes ramming into the Twin Towers on September 11, 2001, for instance, many four- and five-year-olds thought that each time they witnessed this scene, it was a new plane destroying a new building. They couldn't conceive of the concept of replay—something older kids and adults take for granted. When little ones experience fearful or upsetting images they will try to make sense of them, within their limited cognitive abilities. Often they are way off the mark. Children, even up until ages ten or eleven, won't usually say to themselves as they watch a frightening film, "Oh, that is very good makeup, since that monster looks so scary" or "The darkness on the set really makes the scene feel creepy." No, they react to visual images as if they were real, with their emotions engaged intently—not their minds. Consequently, what makes the strongest emotional impact on them is what they will remember most readily. That's why it's a good idea to leave children at home when going out to see a horror film or, if viewing at home, why it makes sense to watch that next *Texas Chainsaw Massacre* movie when the kids are in bed—out of the line of fire, so to speak. Horrific images can linger in young children's minds long after the initial viewing. In fact, research has shown that fears caused by media in childhood can be severe and last well into adulthood. In a 1999 study, 90 percent of college students remembered being intensely scared by something in the media as a child. Young children, children exposed to media presentations depicting blood and injury, and children who did not intend to view the images but went along with others' decisions were most at risk for experiencing enduring fright effects.

As children grow, their fears change. Young children are afraid of the dark and the supernatural, such as ghosts, monsters, and witches, while older kids are usually more afraid of personal injury and harm to those they love. Writing in a 2009 article, Dr. Joanne Cantor, a longtime researcher on this subject, points out that while adolescents also fear personal injury, "school fears and social fears arise at this age, as do fears regarding political, economic, and global issues."

Watching the news can bring up these fears. For instance, a 2006 study, "Children and the War on Iraq: Developmental Differences in Fear Responses to Television News Coverage," showed that thirteen- to seventeen-year-olds reportedly watched more news coverage of the war and experienced greater concern than did children five to eight years old. Consistent with previous research, younger children were more scared by concrete, visual dangers they saw on the news coverage while older kids were more scared by abstract, verbally communicated threats. Despite multiple controls, viewing news about the war in Iraq was a significant and positive predictor of children's heightened safety concerns.

Adults also can become worried about their safety by watching television. George Gerbner, a distinguished researcher, has been studying the content and effects of TV violence on both children and adults for over thirty years. Over that time, he and his colleagues released a significant body of work that showed that a steady diet of violent programming caused both children and adults to see the world and other people as more dangerous than they actually are. He called this effect "the mean world syndrome."

Those who watch five or more hours of television daily are more fearful than those who watch three hours or less. Heavy viewers are more apt to overestimate the chance that they will be victims of crime. They also take more precautions than others, such as limiting their travel at night and changing the security in their homes. They look out for themselves more, trust others less, are more aggressive, and see the possibility of personal harm more often than moderate television viewers.

In a 2013 article, researchers Brad Bushman, Margaret Hall, and Robert Randal summarize the mean world syndrome well: "It is well known that people who consume a lot of violent media come to view the world as a hostile place. People who consume a lot of violent media also think violence is 'normal' behavior, because media characters often use violence to solve their problems."

3. Desensitization to Real-Life and Screen Violence

One mom we know would voice her abhorrence of graphically violent images when she watched TV programs and movies with her teenage sons. They would retort, "Oh Mom, you're just not desensitized enough. You need to see more of this stuff, then it won't affect you so much." Though they said this mostly in jest, the boys were not far from the mark. Research indicates that children may be deliberately trying to conquer their fears of vulnerability and victimization by desensitizing themselves through repeated exposure to horror movies. But to the extent that they desensitize themselves to screen violence and fear, they are also becoming more tolerant of violence in the real world. And more tolerant of themselves as perpetrators of violence.

Often callousness sets in and a "so what?" attitude begins to frame the context of horrific acts, even for real-life violence. The desensitization effect has been called "the bystander effect" because it makes people less empathetic, less likely to react in a prosocial way to helps victims of violence.

Two classic research studies in the 1970s illustrate this. A 1974 study randomly assigned fifth-grade children to watch either fifteen minutes of a television crime drama— including several shootings and other violent acts—or fifteen minutes of a televised baseball game. Afterward, the investigator left each child in charge of supervising the behavior of two younger children by means of a television monitor. "I imagine they'll be okay," they were told. "But sometimes little kids can get into trouble, and that's why an older person should be watching them. If anything does happen, come get me."

After the investigator left, the television monitor showed the two younger children getting into a quarrel, which then escalated into threats and physical blows; finally, the camera was knocked over and, amid shouts and crashing, the monitor went dead. (Unbeknownst to the older children, the fight was taped, not live, so all children witnessed exactly the same sequence.) As compared to the children who had watched the baseball game, the children who had just finished watching fifteen minutes of television violence were five times more likely to simply fail to summon help.

In a seminal study in 1978, Dr. William Belson interviewed 1,565 youths who were representative of thirteen- to seventeen-year-old boys living in London. These boys were interviewed on several occasions concerning the extent of their exposure to a selection of violent TV programs broadcast over a twelve-year period. A BBC viewing panel rated the levels and types of violence. It was thus possible to obtain, for each boy, a measure of both the magnitude and type of exposure to televised violence. Also, each boy's behavior was determined by a self-report indicating involvement in any of fifty-three categories of violence over the previous months. The degree of seriousness of the acts reported by the boys ranged from taunting to more serious and violent behavior. The boys reported atrocities: "I forced a girl to have sexual intercourse with me." "I bashed a boy's head against a wall." "I threatened to kill my father." "I burned a boy on the chest with a cigarette while my mates held him down." After controlling for one hundred other factors, it was found that boys who had watched above-average amounts of television violence were currently engaged in rates of serious violence 49 percent higher than those of boys who had watched below-average quantities of violence.

Now consider that the violence these kids were watching in the seventies was mild by today's standards. Yet, it still affected them in these antisocial ways. So it may be safe to say that graphic violence in today's media, especially in violent video games, desensitizes our kids at even deeper levels. At first, the player may be startled by the blood and the shrieks of agony. He may even mentally or emotionally resist the awful things he's doing to others. But gradually, with repetition, the revulsion recedes. He grows accustomed to the violence and actually will need greater levels of violence—more graphic, more innovative—to begin to feel anything approaching an appropriate reaction. But video games take care of that. Violence levels continually increase, thereby assuring continual desensitization, usually undetected by the player.

Researcher Jeanne Funk, PhD, writing in *Children's Exposure to Violent Video Games and Desensitization to Violence*, provides a good reason for this, "Occurring as an unconscious process over time, desensitization to violence can be defined as the reduction or eradication of cognitive and emotional and . . . behavioral responses to a violent stimulus[;] this . . . desensitization prevents the initiation of moral reasoning processes that normally inhibit aggression."

The Wellington, Ohio, tragedy in 2007 provides a vivid example of absent moral reasoning processes. Daniel Petric, age sixteen, was a big fan of violent, first-person shooter video games, playing them up to eighteen hours a day. His parents, Sue and Mark Petric, tried to get him to stop, but to no avail and finally they chose to take away his favorite, Halo-3.

A few evenings later, Daniel came into the room where his parents were watching TV. Under pretense of saying he had a surprise for them; he asked them to close their eyes. Then with a nine-millimeter handgun taken from his father's lockbox, he shot his mother several times, killing her. He then shot his father in the head (but didn't kill him—unknown at the time to Daniel). Leaving the gun by his father's side, so it might look like a murder-suicide, Daniel collected his beloved Halo-3 game. Soon afterward his sister spotted him in the front of the family van with the game by his side. Evidently, his relationship with the violent video game took precedence over his relationship with his parents

4. Increased Appetite for Violence

Have you noticed that body counts always rise in the sequels to action films? The first *Die Hard* had eighteen deaths; the second 264. The first *RoboCop* had thirty-two deaths, the second eighty-one. This is a typical ploy since a lot of viewers have come to expect increasing amounts of violence in order to feel excited or involved in the action. In an important study published in the November 2013 issue of the journal *Pediatrics*, researcher Brad Bushman and his colleagues found that PG-13 movies today—such as *The Hunger Games* or *The Avengers*—contain more violence than the R-rated films of the 1980s. In particular, gun violence in PG-13 films has tripled since 1985, the year the PG-13 rating was first introduced. And overall, violence in movies has nearly quadrupled since the 1950s.

Dr. Craig Anderson, an internationally renowned researcher calls the rating system "systematic desensitization therapy." Starting with "harmless" PG films that depict cute, cuddly characters inflicting harm while feel-good music plays in the background, it gradually desensitizes youngsters, preparing them for the next level of violence, which they will encounter in PG-13 films. This results in emotionally numb kids who want and expect more intense depictions of violence while feeling less empathy for the suffering of others. Eventually they grow an appetite for violence in order to feel satisfied. Violent entertainment won't be "fun" for them if it doesn't keep escalating.

Hundreds of studies document this effect. The more graphic and realistic the violence, the more kids keep watching. And participating in very realistic portrayals of murder in video games ups the ante because the physiological arousal with its corresponding cascade of hormones keeps the gamer always wanting more.

Evidence can create meaningful changes. We want the scientific evidence about the damaging effects of media violence to begin a public awareness campaign no one can ignore or dismiss. With more time, attention, and resources on media violence as a significant factor contributing to violent behavior by children and teens, we could turn this situation around, perhaps more rapidly than we might think.

THE strides made in understanding smoking as a public health issue serve as a good example. Although the war against tobacco is far from over—four thousand kids try their first cigarette each day—much progress has been made. In the United States we've reduced adult smoking by more than half since the 1960s and youth smoking is now at a record low—under 20 percent. About two-thirds of Americans live in states and communities that require smoke-free restaurants, bars, and other public places. Public attitudes about tobacco have fundamentally changed. And governments worldwide are working to create 100 percent smoke-free enclosed work and public places; to inform the public of the harm caused by tobacco through large and strong pictorial warnings on tobacco packages; and to ban tobacco advertising, promotion, and sponsorship.

We look forward to the day when similar actions are taken around the public health issue of media violence—when so many people believe the scientific evidence about the harmful effects of media violence that we all naturally protect kids from exposure to gratuitous, sensational violent imagery. On that day public attitudes and policies will shift in our kids' favor, and we will finally be able to say, "Yes, the debate is over. The scientific evidence is clear that media violence harms most kids in some way. Now let's roll up our sleeves and do something about it."

CHAPTER THREE

MURDER, TORTURE, BRUTALITY: DANGEROUS "GAMES"

We have made the act of killing and shooting so fun, but we've also taken the importance out of it by piling so much of it in. You don't ever have to think about the concept of pulling a trigger, because even if you run out of bullets, we're going to give you so many more bullets! So many more people to shoot! In fact, even if all the people in the game aren't enough, we're gonna give you Horde mode! You can kill people until you can't kill them anymore!

—Anonymous posting on MetaFilter community weblog

Video game technology continually improves with technological advances, making murder and mayhem increasingly graphic, accessible, and alluring. Realism, the holy grail of the video game industry, enables participation in extremely lifelike representations of murder, torture, and brutality. As graphic as the violence is on TV and in movies, it can't quite compete with a medium where you, not an actor, can control the action. It's a whole new level of involvement—and it can be terrifying to consider the consequences for our kids and for our society as a whole.

For instance, Fallout 3, one of the seven top-selling games of all time, displays "realistic dismemberment" and "slow motion decapitation" while players "use a kitchen knife to kill household members and pets." In Fallout: New Vegas, players can "activate a collar bomb around a slave-woman's neck, resulting in depictions of blood and gore." Diablo III, which sold over 12 million copies worldwide, depicts "battles . . . accompanied by slashing and flesh-impact sounds, screams of pain, and frequent blood-splatter effects . . . some levels depict burning corpses and dead villagers amid large pools of blood."

Ever since the first games came on the market, the advertising focus has been on the realism of the displays. In fact, most reviews of new violent video games also neglect to judge the content while boasting about how good the blood and gore look. It's unnerving that we have come to accept sadism and psychopathic depictions as acceptable recreation. And it's incomprehensible how we have come to allow such "entertainment" for our youth. And things just keep getting worse.

Games for the Wii make the participation more intense. The Godfather: Blackhand Edition, for instance, allows the player to fully immerse himself in the experience through aiming the Wiimote at different enemy body parts in order to choose where the bullet will land. In fact, over fifty executions are possible, demonstrated by detailed on-screen illustrations. A player notes that he is excited about this game because it "adds a new element of depth to the experience, as both the nunchuk and Wii remote become extensions of the player's hands. . . . It's fun to pop a guy in the knee, slowly walk up to him, and put a single revolver shot in his head."

THE steady drip of video game violence throughout kids' days has brainwashed them to enjoy inflicting and reveling in others' pain. And apparently lots of people think acting out murderous rages is fun: Consumers spent a billion dollars in three days after the release of Grand Theft Auto V in 2013. In fact, Grand Theft Auto V entered the Guinness Book of World Records for seven record-breaking achievements, from bestselling video game in twenty-four hours to fastest video game to gross $1 billion. If it were a movie, it would be the highest-grossing movie of all time. While GTA V, like its early renditions, contains plenty of random shooting and senseless mayhem, it also goes a step further by depicting a gruesome waterboarding torture scene, in which the player must choose to continually inflict pain if he wants to advance to the next level. You can't win unless you torture someone. Another disturbing trend in this version of GTA is its outrageous misogyny. In one example, the player takes a drive while listening to the song "Higher Love" by Steve Winwood when a male voice comes on the radio that talks about the value of using a woman as a urinal.

If commercial video games popularize debasement to the lowest common denominator, it is not surprising that young independent game developers are mimicking them and even extending the brutality of their industry role models. For example, in the game Norrland the player experiences killing animals, complete with digital shrieks, and spends a lot of time having bizarre dreams and crashing cars. The game developer, who goes by the code name "Cactus," states, "The game builds toward a climax of compulsive self-loathing and self-destruction, until you finally hang yourself from a tree." He adds, this "is just the kind of idiosyncratic nastiness that video games could use more of."

And that's how it works. Practice murder, torture, and brutality day after day, and a person, especially a kid, can come to want, expect, and seek murder, torture, brutality—and quite possibly then choose to act them out. Perversion will likely prevail on multiple levels in this kid's life—and not only in the video games he plays. There are four important reasons for this. Violent video games are:

- Good at making kids feel satisfied
- Habit forming, even addictive
- Effective teachers and trainers
- Especially good at desensitization

For further understanding, let's examine each of these points in more detail.

Video Games Provide Satisfaction

It's clear that video games are the entertainment of choice for many. In 2011, the PC game market grossed $18.6 billion worldwide. Video game sales in the United States (not including hardware like consoles or accessories) totaled $14.8 billion. And with the face of gaming changing radically, 2012 marked the end of video games as only tangible items sold, rented, or borrowed. Cartridges, Blu-ray discs, and every other format began to make way to downloading. Consequently, in 2012 digital gaming for handheld devices recorded the strongest growth in video games, thanks mainly to the rising use of smartphones and tablets as well as what players considered an improved gaming experience on these devices.

With this explosion of formats, many teens take the

Internet with them wherever they go since 78 percent of teens have smartphones and 23 percent own tablets—a level comparable to the general public—according to a 2013 study. "The nature of teens' Internet use has transformed dramatically—from stationary connections tied to shared desktops in the home to always-on connections that move with them throughout the day," said Mary Madden, senior researcher for the Pew Research Center's Internet Project. Today, violent imagery is with them 24/7, if parents aren't intentionally involved in their children's media use. And although men, with an average age of thirty, are the largest demographic for violent video games, 97 percent of twelve- to seventeen-year-olds and 90 percent of kids ages eight to sixteen in the United States play video games. And since 89 percent of the games are violent, our kids get more than their fair share of horrific violence. And this is true even if they are restricted to teen-rated games only since violent content can be found in 98 percent of "teen-rated" games. It's unfortunate, too, that games rated M (for eighteen and older) seem to tempt a lot of kids to ignore the ratings. Research shows that restrictive age and violent-content labels actually increase the attractiveness of video games for boys and girls of all age groups. And with the growing popularity of massively multiplayer online games (MMOs), well, we could label first-person shooter websites however we like, there's still really nothing to stop a kid with access to a computer, tablet, or smartphone from seeing what's there, communicating with other players, and ordering an array of products. Kids have to get past the manned ticket counter to see restricted films; they have to provide proper identification that they are old enough to buy cigarettes and alcohol; but there are no such obstacles in their way if they want to learn all there is to know about "mature" video games.

Violent or nonviolent, video games in general are good at making us feel good. You probably know a young person who is a serious gamer. These kids will spend most of their waking hours immersed in a game, even when there is no external reward—no one praises them for playing. No one gives them a recognition medal—a common practice now with most kids' sports participation. No one delivers a pizza to their door each time they successfully get to the next level. Yet, without any of these typical types of external rewards, they keep playing. Often oblivious to their surroundings, they may regularly skip meals, living off snacks and energy drinks to ward off sleep in order to keep playing. What is it about a video game that compels such easy investment of time and energy? Is it just for the fun?

Scott Rigby and Richard M. Ryan address this question in their book *Glued to Games: How Video Games Draw Us In and Hold Us Spellbound*. They present a model called the "Player Experience of Needs Satisfaction" (PENS) to explain the draw of video games. The compelling lure is much deeper and more extensive than just "fun." These games satisfy three real, intrinsic human needs that are necessary for psychological health: *autonomy*, *competence*, and *relatedness*.

Autonomy means that we can take action based on our own desires and decisions, not because someone else tells us to do something. Children grow into their autonomous selves one step at a time, gradually learning to direct their own behaviors by making individual choices and evaluating their responses to those choices. *Competence* means we want to develop our skills and experience mastery in new situations. Children and teens practice many skills—such as thinking skills, reading skills, writing skills, life skills, and special talents such as music, sports, and artistic skills—in order to master skills that bring a vital and fulfilling adult life. The third critical intrinsic need, *relatedness*, means we experience ourselves as capable of meaningful connections to others. The ability to relate well is the foundation for all healthy social interactions, supportive friendships, and mature intimacy. Every person needs to experience and develop autonomy, competency, and relatedness because in the long run, a healthy self-identity shrivels up and dies without them. Like feeding vitamins and minerals to the body, competence, autonomy, and relatedness are necessary for a healthy identity.

Over thirty years of research have shown that "when these needs are satisfied, we experience positive feelings and are more motivated to engage in those activities that satisfy us." For instance, a teen might go fishing with some buddies and satisfy these three needs—autonomy, competence, and relatedness—during the outing. In fact the teen might get together with his friends and fish every day during the summer. But chances are he doesn't lose himself in a fishing experience—it's an enjoyable one but not one that comes to take over his life. Usually kids don't lose themselves in everyday experiences. They may love reading, but they still remember to eat. They may be "obsessed" with dance and practice eight hours a day, but they still bathe and see their friends. And they don't lose themselves in the process of enjoying these real-life experiences. So what's different about video games?

Well, let's consider this. A teen might think that he shoots hoops because it's fun and he needs a break from his summer job as a lifeguard. Since his dad played basketball frequently with him when he was young, he has fond memories associated with it. It always made him feel special. So now, when he thinks of shooting a few hoops with his buddies he thinks of fun. Often when he feels a bit out of sorts and needs a pick-me-up, he calls his friends for a game of pickup ball. He always felt capable playing—he's good at it, and he and his dad shared heart-to-heart talks as they played. Basketball supported his needs for autonomy, competence, and relatedness in the past, so consequently it will bring him satisfaction in the present.

Video games also enhance feelings of autonomy, competence, and relatedness—bringing a sense of deep satisfaction to kids when they play them. As Rigby and Ryan note, "compared to many other activities in life, games are remarkably good candidates for need satisfaction, largely because of the *immediacy*, *consistency*, and *density* of intrinsic satisfactions they provide."

With *immediacy*, you can turn to them at a moment's notice for experiences that will engage you in a hero's quest, a historical battle, or a shootout against other players, in running a city simulation or being a thief with no moral restraints who gets to do anything he wants to. It's all there, with a few seconds' notice.

Video games are *consistent*. Once we know how to play them, we can always count on the satisfaction outcome because the rewards follow rules. When we master the challenges embedded in the rules, we will get the rewards. Even if the outcome is that we "get killed" in the game, it is part of mastering the challenges of the game, and "leveling up" to a more challenging part of the game that will provide even greater rewards.

Video games have *density*. That is, their rewards are the satisfaction of autonomy, competence, and relatedness, and these rewards come at a high frequency rate. You don't have to wait a day or a week or a month between rewards. They just keep coming. While in real life it often takes years to develop feelings of personal satisfaction, in video games, fulfillment is around every corner.

All well-designed video games, both violent and nonviolent, provide for needs satisfaction. They do this not through their content, but with their structure and reward system. In violent video games, as Rigby and Ryan remind us, "competence is communicated by immediate and unambiguous positive feedback in response to your actions—you see opponents stagger, see blood fly off them, and ultimately see them collapse. The . . . headshot is particularly effective in this regard." Some games primarily fulfill autonomy needs. Having the option to choose different paths through a level, and different modes or tactics, supports feelings of greater autonomy. Some games include fulfillment of relationship needs along with autonomy or competence. War games, for instance, provide camaraderie, like that of soldiers supporting one another on a battlefield. And some games, such as the massively multiplayer online games (MMOs) and the multiplayer first-person shooter games (multiplayer FPS), fulfill all three psychological needs at the same time. In general, the more needs a game fulfills, the more popular the game will be and the more intense the overall psychological satisfaction.

However, meeting the human needs for autonomy, competence, and relatedness in the virtual world is distinctly different from meeting them in the real world. Needs satisfaction in real life is like eating sugar cane. It tastes sweet, but the taste is not so concentrated, and there are other nutrients in the sugar cane besides sugar. It takes some effort and time to extract the fulfillment of sweetness from chewing on the sugar cane. Needs satisfaction from video games, on the other hand, is like eating a sugar cube. It is concentrated sweetness that you can get just by popping it into your mouth. There is less effort, it happens immediately, and you will always get a known level of satisfaction.

If video games fulfill real psychological needs, how can we help our kids resist seeking all their satisfaction through these games, to the detriment of experiencing feelings of satisfaction and fulfillment in the real world? We need to guide them through an intentional process of video game literacy.

An example from swimming may be useful. There is a difference between swimming in a swimming pool, in a mountain lake, and in an ocean. The swimming pool is not too deep, the water is relatively warm, and the sides are nearby. A mountain lake makes additional demands on the swimmer: The water may be quite cold, so deep you can't touch the bottom, and it's a long way to reach land if you swim very far. Swimming in the ocean can be even more challenging because of large waves and outgoing tides. But an additional challenge, often dangerous to the unwary, is the presence of undertow currents that can pull you under the water. Let's apply these three levels of swimming to the use of screen technologies.

Children usually learn to swim in a swimming pool—starting with the shallow end first. They need to be comfortable in the water and learn the mechanics of swimming first. This could be seen as learning to use screen technologies. Not just the *how*, but also the *why* and the *when*. Hopefully, this is done with educational viewing and child-appropriate movies, with parental guidance. During this swimming-pool stage, the child learns at a rate that is appropriate to her developmental stage. She learns what is okay to watch, how long it's okay to watch, how to balance the viewing with the other activities in her life. She talks with her parents about what she is seeing and learning, and how she feels about it. In this process she is growing self-awareness about her media-related activities.

A child who has already become a good swimmer may go on vacation and swim in a mountain lake. We don't just let him jump in and go swimming by himself. There are dangers there that he doesn't have experience with. He can't reach the bottom. The water is cold and could cause cramps. He may swim out too far and not realize how much effort it will take to swim back to shore. We can liken this to learning to watch TV and movies more critically and using the Internet more responsibly. Parents discuss family values and what is appropriate to watch on TV and in the movies, in relation to what matters most to the family. The child uses the Internet, social media, and his cell phone or tablet more independently, yet with the parents' watchful eye, as he "swims further out from shore." In this way he expands his capacity to self-regulate his media and digital activities and develops his capacity for self-choice within his family values and his community's social norms.

A young person who has learned to swim in a swimming pool, who has met the challenges of swimming in a large, open lake, may spend a summer at the ocean shore. There are new challenges here. Waves can be great fun; they pick you up and carry you. But outgoing tides and undertows can be very dangerous if you are unwary and/or overestimate your swimming ability.

Swimming in the ocean may be likened to playing video games. While many parents may be quite familiar with watching TV, using the Internet, or downloading the latest app, they might not realize that there is something significantly different about video games. Parents are usually not familiar with the "addictive undertow of games." What makes a child or a teen vulnerable to it depends on how much of their needs satisfaction they get from playing video games.

Children and teens without enough fulfilling real-life experiences can use video games as a substitute. Those who already get a healthy dose of needs satisfaction—from school or work activities, from family and friends, from sports and hobbies, from whatever they feel a passionate involvement with—will not find video games as fulfilling. But kids who do not get a healthy level of needs satisfaction from their daily lives will be more vulnerable to actually needing these games to feel satisfied. Kids who live unsatisfying lives gravitate to the thrills of the virtual world. Rigby and Ryan summarize it this way: "It is for those who have a strong contrast between an unsatisfying life and a highly satisfying virtual world where we believe a strong risk for overuse is present. It is when this combination of factors come together that gamers can really get sucked in and stuck in game worlds." The authors further note that there is a kind of double whammy to this situation: "When an individual's daily life is characterized by less satisfaction or more frustration of basic needs, they are both more likely to be vulnerable to an obsessive focus on activities that are somewhat need satisfying, and they will be less able to control that passion." That may explain why so many kids love playing video games at the expense of experiencing real life—video games make them feel more satisfied and fulfilled than living in the world of their current reality. And for a lot of kids whose lives are in shambles it is easy to see how video games can come to their rescue.

Violent Video Game Addiction

It's important that we not stereotype compulsive gamers. They are not social outcasts who come from homes where they didn't get their basic needs met. Often they are very capable people. In their research Scott Rigby and Richard Ryan noted that these folks "fall in love with what the real world doesn't offer—a high density of psychological need satisfactions that come from being a hero, accomplishing goals, and teaming up with friends to accomplish epic feats."

An instructive example of such a person is Dr. Andrew P. Doan, the author of the intriguing book *Hooked on Games: The Lure and Cost of Video Game and Internet Addiction*, his personal story of his gaming addiction. Dr. Doan was caught in the undertow of video game play and, by his own acknowledgment, almost drowned. He describes the process of entrapment, and what it took to escape, with great insight, including the perspective gained from his medical and scientific training. Dr. Doan is a practicing ophthalmologist with a PhD in neuroscience, and his story demonstrates clearly that if he could get hooked, anyone can.

Of course, just playing games a lot does not make it an addiction. Clinically, for something to qualify as an addiction, it has to make you dysfunctional in multiple areas of your life. If playing games is significantly affecting your relationship with your family, if your grades are becoming poor in school, or if your work on your job is being neglected, and social relationships (except with other gamers) are falling by the wayside, then it is clinically correct to call it an addiction. How many of our kids fall into this category?

Several studies have been done to estimate the size of the subgroup of gamers who play almost constantly, obsessively seeking immersion in the game. Estimates vary, but various studies across several nations suggest that it could be as much as 10 to 15 percent. In the introduction to Dr. Doan's book *Hooked on Games*, Dr. Douglas Gentile, describes one study done in the United States that included 1,100 eight- to eighteen-year-olds. He started with the assumption that he would not find very many people who fit the clinical definition of addiction. He was surprised when he "found that 8.5 percent would classify as pathological gamers by this [clinical] definition. . . . There are about forty million children between eight and eighteen years old in the United States. Approximately 90 percent of them play video games. If 8.5 percent of them are pathological, that's over 3 million children seriously damaging multiple areas of their lives because of their gaming habits!"

It is appalling that something this pervasive hasn't garnered more public outcry. Hilarie Cash and Kim McDaniel may give us a clue why in their book *Video Games & Your Kids*. They observe that: "South Korea and China have declared video game addiction their most pressing public health concern. Video game addiction is minimized in America, perhaps because it remains hidden within individual households. We do not have the widespread cultural phenomenon of cyber cafes where gaming is conducted in public. Where this is the custom, the tragedies that occur are public as well."

We might observe that in the United States, we have a very well funded industry voice that focuses on debunking concerns about violent video games, because science hasn't "really" proved anything yet. If we had a viral outbreak that significantly affected over 3 million children, would there be a public clamor to find the cause and remedy it as soon as possible? To the video game industry, there is no such thing as pathological playing. In their view, if "a few" players suffer from a little overplaying, then maybe that is just a little "collateral damage" in reaching the goal of greater profits. Unfortunately that "collateral damage" is over 3 million of our kids.

Parents are alarmed at not just the violent images in the games but at the amount of time their children spend playing them. More than 60 percent of children and teens report that they play video games longer than they intend to play. And since screens saturate our kids' lives at increasingly younger ages, we can expect this number to increase. For instance, studies in 2012 show toddlers and preschoolers interacting with iPads and smartphones for up to two hours daily. When screen time replaces necessary developmentally appropriate activities such as playing in the 3-D world, more children will find the lure of screen technologies hard to resist. We see this already happening. A growing number of children as young as four years old require psychological treatment to break their already-entrenched screen habit. Yet research shows that by the time children turn ten years old, every additional hour of screen time as toddlers is associated with lower math and school achievement, reduced physical activity, and increased victimization in middle school. Add to this equation that many five- to eight-year-olds now play violent video games with well-intentioned but misguided parents who view this as an appropriate bonding experience with their children, and we face an impending disaster for families, schools, and society. The fact is the earlier children start with screen technologies, the more difficult it will be for them to resist violent video games as they grow.

It's no surprise that violent video games are habit forming and require thought and discipline to resist. The interactive quality, the intensity of the violence, the physiological reactions all serve to connect the player's feelings of exhilaration and accomplishment directly to the violent images. And "good" feelings keep the player wanting to play. Countless parents try desperately to keep video game play within certain time limits, but it's a huge challenge . . . a parental battle we often lose. Once kids get hooked, it's difficult to unhook them. And with more online gaming requiring a subscription to play, kids can succumb easily to conditioning tactics, often used intentionally by the game makers.

This controversial practice has made gaming techniques more overtly behavioristic in nature, blatantly providing elements of stimulus-response to keep people playing and, of course, paying. A prominent independent developer, Jonathan Blow, went as far as to call these games, such as World of Warcraft, unethical and exploitative:

"I think a lot of modern game design is actually unethical, especially massively multiplayer games like World of Warcraft, because [developers] string them along with little pieces of candy so that they'll suffer through terrible game play, but keep playing because they gain levels or new items. . . . That kind of reward system is very easily turned into a Pavlovian or Skinnerian scheme. It's considered best practice: schedule rewards for your player so that they don't get bored and give up on your game. That's actually exploitation."

Video games, in general, make extensive use of reinforcement schedules for both the acquisition and maintenance of the habit. According to Jane Healey, in her classic book *Endangered Minds*, there are four basic elements that make video games so habit forming:

1. The player experiences feelings of mastery and control. The less sense of power the child or teen feels in his or her life, the more this element may become important as an addictive factor. (In fact, studies show that generally boys' preferences for violent video games are associated with low self-competence—in school, in personal relationships, and in general behavior. For girls, more time playing video or computer games is associated with lower self-esteem.)

2. The level of play is exactly calibrated to the player's ability level. Rather than coping with the challenging problems in the real world, young people are easily drawn into following the more made-to-order sequence in video games.

3. The player receives immediate and continual reinforcement, which make the games particularly addictive.

4. The player can escape life and be immersed in a constructed reality that seems to be totally in his or her control. (We all know that one of the anxieties of being young is a lack of control. Parents, teachers, clergy, and caregivers tell you what to do, and it's not always very much fun. It's one reason why children have active imaginations and like to construct their own worlds. And it's usually healthy for them to do so—if they are exercising their own imagination. Video game manufacturers understand this desire—and they give kids all the things they want, for as long as they're willing to stick with the game.)

"A definite drug response" is how Dr. Donald Shifrin, a pediatrician and the American Academy of Pediatrics representative on the National Television Violence Study, describes what he sees when children and teens play video games at home. "When youngsters get into video games the object is excitement. The child then builds a tolerance for that level of excitement. Now the child mimics drug-seeking behavior . . . initially there's experimentation, behavior to seek the drug for increasing levels of excitement, and then there is habituation, when more and more of the drug is actually necessary for these feelings of excitement. . . . If parents want, rent a video game for a day and then return it. Everyone goes to Disneyland for a day. No one goes there daily."

Are children and teens who regularly play violent video games in a permanent state of arousal? We know that merely watching violent imagery physiologically arouses both children and adults. Early experiments using physiological measures of arousal such as galvanic skin response, heart rate, and respiratory changes found that children are emotionally responsive to even animated television violence. If being a spectator to the sensational arouses our children, what happens when they get to engage in the simulated slaughter?

The effects of violent video games on teens and young adults' arousal levels, hostile feelings, and aggressive thoughts have been measured. Important research by Dr. Craig Anderson and Dr. Karen Dill found that college students who had played a violent virtual reality game had a higher heart rate, reported more dizziness and nausea, and exhibited more aggressive thoughts in a posttest than those who had played a nonviolent game. Other studies show differences in cardiovascular reactions and hostility following violent video game play, producing "numerous changes in the body," including increased heart rates, higher blood pressure, and increased skin conductance.

Dr. Andrew Boylan summarized data that researchers have found over the last decade to show how physiological arousal can have significant effects long after the video game is finished. In a 2013 paper presented at the National

Communication Association Convention, "Arousal and Aggressive Response over Time: Excitation Transfer in Graphic Video Games," Dr. Boylan explains a process called "excitation transfer." This describes what happens when a player who has been aroused by playing violent video games transfers his aggression to real-life annoyances, often blowing situations out of proportion. "The player acts more aggressively—due to heightened arousal—in a situation where he or she otherwise would not." And to make matters worse, this ongoing state of hyper excitation limits normal brain activity. A 2010 groundbreaking study led by Dr. Jordan Grafman, senior investigator at the National Institute of Neurological Disorders and Stroke, found that "continued exposure to violent videos will make an adolescent less sensitive to violence, more accepting of violence, and more likely to commit aggressive acts, since the emotional component associated with aggression is reduced and normally acts as a brake on aggressive behavior."

Since kids repetitively practice violence while in a high state of arousal and derive deep psychological satisfaction from this practice, significant conditioning processes occur in violent video game play. The chart on the following page shows the three levels of this conditioning. At the ground-floor level, the child's brain wires neurological circuits that associate feelings of satisfaction with inflicting pain on others. At the psychological level, a sense of self develops that, with practice, becomes more comfortable with being able to inflict pain on other people. And, at the sociological level, the implicit conditioning is that it is normal to feel okay about inflicting pain on other people.

Multi-Level Conditioning from Practicing Video Game Violence

Sociological Level	It is *normal* to feel OK about inflicting pain on other people.
Psychological Level	A sense of self that is *comfortable with being able* to inflict pain on other people.
Neurological Level	Wiring neuro circuits that *associate feelings of satisfaction* with inflicting pain on other people.

Conditioning kids like this may be a costly social experiment. Through violent video game play, we condition our kids to expect satisfaction from others' discomfort and pain, to be more comfortable with harming others, and to think that it's okay to hurt others—a recipe for disaster we see currently being played out in the current crisis of youth bullying and cyberbullying.

And what they're not doing may be as important as what they are. As children and teens play violent video games for twenty to forty hours weekly, they are not solving and negotiating conflicts with their peers, and they are missing priceless opportunities to gain needed cooperative learning and social skills in the real world. Instead, the world constructed for them by video game manufacturers comes to determine their ability to deal with people in the real world. The more inept they become at communicating cooperatively with actual people, the more likely it is that they will lose themselves in the video games, particularly violent ones that ensure feelings of control, mastery, and exhilaration. And then, as the real world of slowness and struggle, decisions and demands becomes less appealing, the more violent video games interfere with children's healthy psychological and physiological development.

Violent Video Games Are Effective Teachers and Trainers

If you want to perfect a skill, what's the first thing you have to be willing to do? Practice, of course. Because video games have built-in satisfaction and conditioning aspects, practice becomes a breeze. Parents seldom have to coax their kids to practice their video games. Right? Kids do so quite willingly—often in stark contrast to the prodding they need to get their homework done or remember to practice piano. These activities take a certain amount of patience with a slow-moving thinking process. Video games are easy by comparison. Since the ease of video game playing means plenty of practice, kids are continually exposed to video games' excellent teaching techniques.

Research has demonstrated that video games can teach skills helpful in real-world situations. For instance, one study showed that having played three or more hours of video games a week was a better predictor of a laparoscopic surgeon's skills than his or her level of surgical training. Video games can teach diabetic kids how to take better care of themselves. A study showed that video game health learning decreased kids' diabetes-related urgent and emergency

VIOLENT VIDEO GAMES: YOUR CHILD'S FAVORITE TEACHER

Video games use techniques that are very effective learning tools. Video games:

- Give clear objectives. There isn't confusion about the purpose of learning.
- Effectively adapt to the child's prior knowledge. The child is always in a comfortable learning zone—not too hard, not too easy.
- Pace the child according to his or her skill level, with levels of increasing difficulty so the child experiences competence before the next challenge. The child feels competent and autonomous before new learning is introduced.
- Provide practice, immediate feedback, and more practice based on that feedback. The child's feelings of competence and autonomy increase.
- Reinforce both extrinsically (with points, better weapons, more money, etc.) and intrinsically (advancement to higher levels of complexity). As the child's sense of belonging increases as he "levels up," he is more motivated to keep learning through the video game.
- Go beyond mastery to overlearning, so that knowledge and skills become automatized and consolidated in memory. The child can now retrieve the knowledge and skills learned easily and quickly to use in new situations.

Adapted from "Violent Video Games as Exemplary Teachers: A Conceptual Analysis," by Douglas A. Gentile and J. Ronald Gentile, *Journal of Youth and Adolescence,* vol. 9 (2008), pp. 127–41. Also available at www.DrDouglas.org. Used with permission.

visits by 77 percent after six months. In another study, playing the 2010 active Wii game Rayman Raving Rabbids helped dyslexic kids learn to focus their attention, making it easier for them to learn to read. The researchers concluded, "Nine days on the Wii equaled a year of traditional therapy."

Denying that playing violent video games teaches our kids to enjoy hurting others just doesn't make sense. Military video games provide an informative illustration.

These games satisfy all three of the psychological needs—helping kids feel competent, autonomous, and related to their "buddies." The games actually create bonds among team members that are akin to those created in actual "bands of brothers" that have fought together in real wars. What do our kids learn when they play these games? Perhaps some military history will be useful.

The military learned in World War II that there is a vast gulf between being an ordinary citizen and being someone who can aim and fire a gun at another human being with intent to kill, even in war. They discovered that firing at bull's-eye targets in training did not properly prepare soldiers for combat. Bull's-eye targets are not humans. Shooting at a bull's-eye target may teach someone the mechanics of aiming a gun, pulling the trigger, and dealing with the recoil, but it doesn't teach what it takes to look at another human being, lift up a weapon, and knowingly try to take his life. Soldiers in that war spent a lot of time firing their guns into the air or not at all. In fact, the firing rate was a mere 15 percent among riflemen, which, from a military perspective, is like a 15 percent literacy rate among librarians.

The introduction of training simulators changed history.

It began with flight simulators and tank crew simulators half a century ago, then progressed to shooting simulators. The army's first simulators used "simulated people" or silhouettes as targets, and that appears to have been sufficient to increase the firing rate manyfold. Their introduction is undeniably responsible for increasing the firing rate from 15 to 20 percent in World War II to 95 percent in Vietnam. In the Falklands War, the Argentine soldiers, trained to fire at bull's-eye targets, had a firing rate of approximately 10 to 15 percent. The British, trained to kill using modern methods, had well over a 90 percent firing rate. Thus we know that, all other factors being equal, 75 to 80 percent of the killing on the modern battlefield is a direct result of training with simulators.

There are three things you need in order to shoot and kill effectively and efficiently. From a soldier in Vietnam to an eleven-year-old in Jonesboro, anyone who does not have all three will essentially fail in any endeavor to kill. First, you need a gun. Next you need the skill to hit a target with that gun. And finally you need the will to use that gun. The gun, the skill, and the will. Of these three factors, the military knows that the killing simulators take care of two out of three by nurturing both the skill and the will to kill a fellow human being.

Improved technology now allows the military and the police to train on computer simulators—to learn how to shoot, where to shoot, how to maneuver through possibly deadly combat situations, how to tell enemy from friend, and, most important, how to kill. The entire event of killing in combat can now be simulated by a computer. The primary value of this simulation is in developing the will to kill by repeatedly rehearsing the act until it feels natural.

Now these simulators are in our homes—in the form of violent video games!

Operant conditioning is a very powerful procedure of stimulus-response training, which gives a person the skill to act under stressful conditions. A benign example is the use of flight simulators to train pilots. Airline pilots in training sit in front of a flight simulator for endless, mind-numbing hours; they are taught to react in a certain way when a particular stimulus warning light goes on. When another warning light goes on, a different reaction is necessary. Stimulus-response, stimulus-response, stimulus-response. One day they are actually flying a jumbo jet, the plane is going down, and three hundred people are screaming behind them. They're scared out of their wits, but they do the right thing. Why? Because they've been conditioned to respond in a particular way to this crisis situation. They react from a conditioned response rather than making a cerebral decision. Thinking too much in these types of situations may mean that you will be dead before you do something effective.

It's safe to say that such technology is much more dangerous in the hands of kids than among soldiers and cops—the examples from chapter 1 illustrate that, as does common sense. There often are no safeguards at home and in arcades, no supervision, nor anyone around to put this technology into perspective for a child. In the military and law enforcement worlds, the right option is often *not* to shoot, and recruits receive extensive training about this. Often, recruits are reprimanded, punished, or even "failed" and kicked out for making too many mistakes—that is, for shooting the wrong targets or for shooting without authorization. But when a kid plays

Comparison of Basic Training

ITEM OF COMPARISON	MILITARY/POLICE TRAINING	CHILDREN/TEEN TRAINING
Age That Training Can Start	Military: 18. Police: In 20s, often after completion of military service.	About 8 to 18.
Stage of Brain Development	Near end of brain growth, with connections to prefrontal cortex fairly well developed.	Brain is still growing. Connections between limbic brain and prefrontal cortex often not yet developed.
Context of Training	Under rigorous discipline, with immediate response to authority.	Little or no adult supervision. Little or no feedback on what is learned.
Uses Violent Video Games to Train Shooting Skills	YES	YES
Purpose of Video Games	Adjunct to real-world training.	Training not designed *for* transfer to the real world, BUT training not designed to *inhibit* transfer to the real world.
Trained to Shoot Accurately, Quickly	YES	YES
Trained in Real-World Consequences of Shooting	YES	NO
Trained When NOT to Shoot	YES	NO
Trained in WHO to shoot	Targets must be identified.	Targets are often anyone available.
Disciplined for Shooting Without Authority	YES (harshly disciplined)	NO

a video game, there is *always* the intention to shoot. *There is never an incentive not to shoot.* (See Comparison of Basic Training on the following page.) And there's always some stimulus to keep excitement high, heart rate up, thinking functions closed down. This process is extraordinarily powerful. The result is more homemade pseudo-sociopaths who kill reflexively, even when they don't intend to. Across America we are reaping the bitter harvest of this "training" as ever more kids shoot their girlfriends or their teachers or other individuals they have grudges against. A horrific aspect of this development is that rather than just stopping with their intended target, these kids keep firing—and a simple grudge turns into a mass murder. The point is, these games are indeed affecting our children, and we can't hide behind the myriad other excuses when kids "go off." Because when they do, they do so in all the ways these games train them to—to kill every living person in front of them until they run out of bullets or run out of targets. That results in a lot of dead bodies.

Michael Carneal, the fourteen-year-old boy who walked into a West Paducah school and opened fire on a prayer group meeting that was breaking up, never moved his feet during his rampage. He never fired far to the right or left, never far up or down. He simply fired once at everything that popped up on his "screen." It is not natural to fire once at each target. The normal, almost universal, response is to fire at a target until it drops and then move on to the next target. This is the defensive reaction that will save our lives, the human instinctual reaction—eliminate the threat quickly. Not to shoot once and then go on to another target before the first threat has been eliminated. But most video games teach you to fire at each target only once, hitting as many targets as you can as fast as you can in order to rack up a high score. Modern games teach a more "realistic" skill of shooting until the target drops. And as we know, a lot of video games give bonus effects for head shots. It's awful to note that of Michael Carneal's eight shots he had eight hits, all head and upper torso, three dead and one paralyzed with a .22 caliber pistol—one of the smallest and least effective calibers. To get such deadly effectiveness with that gun takes remarkable skill. Yet, Carneal shot with great accuracy despite the fact that prior to stealing the pistol, he had never shot a real handgun in his life.

If Carneal had been trained by a human being on how to use a handgun properly, he would not have shot in this way.

Violent Video Games Are Especially Good at Desensitization

You probably know about and may even have experienced the benefits of using video games as effective desensitization tools. Fear of spiders? Not a problem. You can immerse yourself in a virtual world, feeling spiders crawling over you and in time, you won't mind it. Same goes for fear of flying. It's all about rehearsal. Climb aboard and take your seat, buckle up, gaze out the window and take off—hundreds of times a day. It's only "make believe," but eventually you'll be able to get on an actual plane without cajoling from others, without forcing yourself. You will walk calmly on board, take your seat, buckle up, gaze out the window, and take off, "comfortably numb" (as Pink Floyd might say). Violent video games work in the same way to systematically desensitize through rehearsal. Rehearse shooting, killing, maiming, and hurting others in countless ways, hundreds of times a day and you are bound to repress empathy. The research couldn't be clearer. Citing a summary of the American Psychological Association's studies in a 2013 article, Mike Jaccarino writes "when one combines all relevant empirical studies using meta-analytic techniques . . . five separate effects emerge with considerable consistency. Violent video games are significantly associated with: increased aggressive behavior, thoughts and affect; increased physiological arousal and decreased prosocial (helping) behavior."

Let's face it, with violent video games kids rehearse being both psychopaths and sadists. Delroy L. Paulhus, a psychology professor at the University of British Columbia explains the distinction. "Psychopaths want to get things from people and don't care about hurting them to do so. . . . Sadists look for opportunities to hurt people, and prolong it for their own pleasure." We play a dangerous game with our kids' hearts and minds if we allow them to play these "games." Hearts become desensitized when minds stop making connections. This is the psychopathic part. Where does a conscience come from? The lower brain with its survival mechanism, quick to react to any perceived threat, can't help us here. It's the developed mind with a well-equipped imagination that gives us the capacity for compassion. When we say to a child, "Imagine what it's like to be homeless," the first prerequisite is that the child must have an imagination. In order to have any inkling of a homeless person's plight, the child must have a thinking function for understanding and an imaginative ability for visualization. And those capacities cannot and will not develop as our children play violent video games because as they mindlessly murder others, they are not generating images in their heads of connecting empathically with the victims. Youth killers often feel absolutely nothing—not a trace of emotion—as they murder others. Relentlessly rehearsing killing in the virtual world, they have distanced themselves emotionally from their victims—thousands of times—just like folks emotionally distance themselves from fear of spiders or from fear of flying when conditioned by video games to do so.

Once the brain disconnects from empathy, it solidifies the link between pleasure and violence. Rehearsing violent video games is a two-way street. A set of neural pathways shut down empathy; other neural pathways ramp up the pleasure of hurting others. This is the sadistic part. Ask any kid why s/he plays video games and nine times out of ten you'll get the answer, "'Cause it's fun." Then ask, "What's fun about killing (maiming, stabbing, etc.) others?" And usually, the response is, "Don't know." Of course they don't know. It's just fun, that's all. We are not hearing the child's thoughts expressed. The endorphins talk because they remember. The thrill of participating in the on-screen violence becomes a sought-after, repeatable rush. Columbine was horrifying. Yet there were many youths who wanted to, and tried to (and some who succeeded) in imitating that level of rampage violence. There were even adults who made and played the video game Super Columbine Massacre RPG! (2005), which reenacted in detail the grisly scenarios, if you can believe that.

We have to be careful. The increasing number of "normal" youths killing and expressing the abnormal desire to kill other human beings may be desensitizing all of us. Dr. George Drinka, a child and adolescent psychiatrist, and the author of *When Media Is the Parent*, makes this astute observation: "We fail to take a closer look at how the society has hardened itself to such slaughter. . . . We may see this all as fictional, but this blood-splashed imagery has seeped, I suggest, deeply into our sensibilities as a people."

WHAT'S the purpose of violent video games in the lives of our children and teens, anyway? Do violent video games make our kids more human and humane? Or do they do just the opposite?

Jaron Lanier, a computer scientist and one of the pioneers in virtual reality, reminds us, "The most important thing about a new technology is how it changes people." Our children are changing with the technology—how could they not be?—as they wander through cyberspace mutilating and killing everything in their path, and having a great time doing it. As they rehearse psychopathic and sadistic behaviors in the virtual world, they limit their time practicing empathy, cooperation, and compassion in the real one.

And what will happen when Wii games get more sophisticated so the "blood" will spurt around your living room in holographic goblets? And how will we react as our kids don glasses or ear implants and escape totally into their virtual world of violence? How far does the technology of killing have to advance before we say "Enough already"?

CHAPTER FOUR

THE STORY I TELL
MYSELF ABOUT MYSELF

Self-identity is inextricably bound up with the identity
of the surroundings.

—Lars Svendsen, *A Philosophy of Boredom*

For months, the seven-year-old boy went to sleep, night
after night, with DVDs from the *Nightmare on Elm
Street* series. The boy knew Freddy Krueger well. When
the Canadian researcher queried him for a study on media
violence's effect on children, she began by asking, "Weren't
you afraid? Didn't Freddy Krueger scare you?" "Oh yes, at
first I was really, really scared," the boy replied. "Then I
just started pretending to be Freddy Krueger and I wasn't
afraid. Now, that's what I always do and I'm never scared
anymore."

Here is an illustrative example of a young child trying
to make sense of what terrifies him. He desperately needs
to figure out how to be more in control of his fear and

anxiety in order to cope. So he does something about it—according to his immature analytic abilities. By pretending to be Freddy Krueger, he arrives at a suitable solution for himself, although it may sadden, and even frighten, us. Obviously, how children's brains decide to interpret what they see on the screen may not be the best or most accurate choice. Within their budding cognitive framework, they will interpret what they see in ways that make sense to them but may astound the adults around them. If we don't ask kids how they are interpreting media images, we will never know how they filter them through limited lenses. And we sure won't be able to intervene appropriately, in case they are identifying strongly with the violent character, as this boy did with Freddy Krueger. Dr. Alvin Poussaint, professor of psychiatry at Harvard Medical School, has stated that exposing children to violent media images is "abuse" similar in effect to physical or sexual abuse or living in a war zone. "None of us," says Dr. Poussaint, "would willingly put a child into those situations, yet we do not act to keep them from watching movies about things we would be horrified to have them see off the screen."

Studies find that often kids will relate easily to the perpetrators of the violence. They want to be and act like them. Researcher Brad Bushman, PhD, and his colleagues examined what they call "wishful identification." In one experimental study nine- and ten-year-old boys played a violent video game and rated how much they identified with the game's character. Afterward they competed on a task with another boy where the winner could blast the loser through loud headphones. They were told that the highest noise levels (i.e., 8, 9, or 10) could cause permanent hearing damage. Although this was not true, the boys did not know it. The findings showed just how much the antics of the video game perpetrator impressed them. The boys who identified with the violent character did in fact administer potentially damaging noise blasts. It was noted in the study that "during the debriefing, one boy said, 'I blasted him with level 10 noise because he deserved it. I know he can get hearing damage, but I don't care.'" Another boy said he liked the violent game "because in this game you can kill people and shoot people, and I want to do that, too." A third boy said, "I like Grand Theft Auto a lot because you can shoot at people and drive fast in cars. When I'm older I can do these things too. I would love to do all these things right now!"

In the violent video games, the boys discovered blanket permission to imitate aggressive behaviors. And when they become more aggressive in their daily lives, chances are they will seek out more aggressive media, which in turn will make them more aggressive, creating a self-reinforcing cycle. Dr. Bushman calls this the "downward spiral" model of aggression and media effects. Writing in the *Washington and Lee Law Review*, he and his colleague Jodi Whitaker explain, "the more the child identifies with the observed character, and the more the observed behavioral scripts are rewarded and deemed appropriate, the more firmly these scripts will be embedded in the child's mind."

Now consider the example of the seven-year-old going to bed at night pretending to be Freddy Krueger. The story of Freddy Krueger is the story he tells himself about himself.

The attitudes and behaviors—the scripts that make up Freddy's repertoire—become an integral part of the young boy's script about himself. And, because the outcome of being Freddy Krueger is positive—he survives while others don't—Freddy's violent and antisocial behavior gets firmly embedded into the boy's script about himself.

Bushman's research clearly demonstrates that a child who has uncritically taken into his sense of self a script of violent behavior that he perceives to work for him will be a child whose self-identity is understood as a violent perpetrator—and that sense of self is not easily changed.

A HEALTHY SELF-IDENTITY
GROWS OVER TIME

Consider these two scenarios:

Bobby's mom just called for him—for the fifth time—but he hasn't heard her. He's so immersed in the video game he's playing that he's blocked out everything else. His mom has to tap him on the shoulder and physically turn him around to face her to get him to stop and listen to her. "I made your favorite, spaghetti and meatballs and garlic bread—take a whiff, you can smell it clear upstairs. The bread just came out of the oven." Bobby isn't paying attention; he's already back to the game. She has to coax him to stop, promising him more time to play after dinner, against her instincts. It's a major hassle. But he knows she won't leave without him, so he finally tears himself away and follows her downstairs cussing loudly all the way. After dinner, Bobby, age twelve, rushes back for another three hours of video game playing before his dad has to make him stop by pulling the plug and taking the system out of his bedroom. It's way past Bobby's bedtime and it's a school night.

Across the cul-de-sac, Bobby's neighbor, Alex, also twelve, plays his favorite video game. His mom has just called him for dinner. "Down in a minute," he yells. "Oh, boy, and I was just getting to the next level," he complains to himself. In less than three minutes Alex has made a decision to stop playing and go down for dinner. Why? The alluring aromas of meatloaf and biscuits filling the air make him suddenly realize that he is very hungry. After dinner, Alex goes back for a half hour of playing the game and then he quits. He is done for the night. Feeling an urgent need to move, Alex goes out in the driveway and shoots some hoops until dark. He comes in, has a snack, and reads for a while until bedtime—the new science fiction novel he has started is just getting good. His parents have to remind him of lights out or he would read late into the night.

BOBBY and Alex, both twelve, play video games—nonviolent ones. Alex is responsible and has skills to resist the lure of video games. When he plays the games he still has a sense of what's going on around him. Even though he was in the middle of "leveling up" when his mom calls him for dinner, she only has to call him once. He smells the food and is eager to get to it. He knows what his needs are and how to fulfill them. For instance, he senses when his body needs to move and has something he enjoys doing physically. He obviously is motivated to do other things besides play video games. He is a reader who can get engrossed in a book.

Bobby, on the other hand, becomes so swept away in video game play that he is oblivious to his mother's calls for dinner. When he finally breaks away, he does so reluctantly with anger. Bobby's life revolves around video games—he has nothing else that gives him this much pleasure, not even eating. He doesn't meet his own needs well and is on the path to a full-blown video game addiction.

We have talked about the types of risk and protective factors that work together to determine whether a child will act more like Alex or more like Bobby. An additional protective factor is a healthy self-identity. Alex has it. Bobby does not.

Alex's self-identity reflects a self-understanding that allows for sound decision making. His sense of self allows him to be self-regulated appropriately for his age. He can control himself—his parents don't have to control him. He knows what his needs are and, consequently, he makes good decisions for himself. Put another way, Alex possesses a healthy self-identity which can be defined as *the ability to make decisions from a source within oneself with clarity about one's skills, talents, values, and needs*.

Self-identity, one of the creative marvels of the human brain, comes from a complex process that intertwines elements from the child's growing body, elements from developing neural systems and the biochemistry of hormonal systems, elements from psychological traits, and elements from social relationships. The process probably begins during prenatal development and continues throughout childhood and adolescence.

This self-identity is truly a *sensed* self-identity. Because the process begins before we are conscious of ourselves as unique individuals, different from others in the external world, the foundations of our self-identity lie in the unconscious processes of the brain. We never have a fully developed, clearly articulated "blueprint" drawing of our self-identity. It is usually fuzzy, often with unknown boundaries, until some experience forces us to say, "I am this; I am not that." As we continually make the distinction between who we are and who we are not, we acquire our values, priorities, and a sense of purpose and meaning in life. These guide children in intentionally growing a conscious self-identity. With maturity we're fairly certain we know who we are and what we're about—most of the time. Life's challenges give us choices that lead us to continually question that certainty. We may be clear about something one day and conflicted or ambivalent the next. Even as adults, we must continually return to who we think we are to determine if our decisions "fit" within that understanding of ourselves.

There are two important considerations about our sense of self-identity we need to understand to fully grasp how media violence impacts it. The first relates to how much of our brain processing is unconscious. In the emerging field of social neuroscience, *unconscious mind* has a new meaning. It does not refer to something that is repressed, like the Freudian unconscious. Instead, as Leonard Mlodinow points out in his book *Subliminal: How Your Unconscious*

Mind Rules Your Behavior, "mental processes are thought to be unconscious because there are portions of the mind that are inaccessible to consciousness due to the architecture of the brain. . . . The inaccessibility of the new unconscious is not considered to be a defense mechanism, or unhealthy. It is considered normal." Some 95 percent of all brain processing is unconscious. That means violent imagery is being processed unconsciously in the brains of children—they are unaware of its influences, but its effects can be seen in attitudes and behaviors, especially over time.

The second important consideration is the fact that the brain of the child is not a miniature version of the adult brain. Although the child's heart is a miniature replica of an adult heart and the lungs tiny versions of future adult lungs, a child's brain is an organ that will change considerably as it matures over the course of childhood and adolescence. In fact, new research indicates that the brain is not fully mature until about age twenty-three or twenty-five. As the developing brain builds neural structures for optimal activity, it is very vulnerable to stimuli from the environment. A lack of the proper kinds of stimuli, combined with the wrong kind of stimuli at inappropriate times, can cause an increased risk to the harmful effects of media violence.

Influences on Self-Identity

A child learns about herself first from her parents, then from the people around her, like relatives and teachers, and then through people in the larger community, like a camp counselor or a soccer coach. In the process of learning about herself through personal relationships, she also learns about herself through society's messages. At age five, for instance, she may witness a 5K run for breast cancer and understand that this is an important issue for women and possibly for her one day. As she grows she will absorb messages from the people who love her and who are personally connected to her, along with messages from her experiences in the larger world.

In a mass media culture such as ours, each sphere of influence in a child's life is impacted by mass media messages as well. Would that parents could influence their children without media interference! Not possible. The media has been called "the third parent" because of its pervasive, repetitive, and constant presence in the lives of our children. Mass media actually "comes between" and impacts every personal and societal relationship our children form. It's ever present. Inescapable.

Images, ideas, attitudes, and trends amplified through the mass media delivery systems of TV, movies, and video games can replace existing norms with a new set of values that embrace destruction, violence, and death as a daily focus. Ideally, we'd live in a larger culture that affirms the morals, values, attitudes, and behaviors we personally teach our children—a culture that mirrors our parental voice—but we don't. Mass media messages, including violent ones, join us in telling our kids who they are and who they can become. This influence is pervasive at every juncture in a child's life. In fact, as spheres of influence expand with the child's growth, mass media's effects become stronger

Spheres of Influence for a Child's Growth

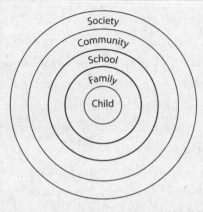

The child's sense of self-identity starts with the parent-child bond, and is held within the family. As the child grows, self-identity moves into larger, overlapping spheres of influence. From the relationships and experiences encountered in these spheres of influence, the child absorbs and chooses experiences and images of (1) what is **possible** to include in its sense of identity, and (2) what is **appropriate** to include.

Copyright © 2013 Gloria DeGaetano. Used with permission.

because they are amplified through all relationships in each sphere of influence.

Now, along with the external influences from family, school, community, and mass media, there are also internal sources of influence on a child's self-identity. These sources, mostly unconscious, interact with the external sources. Let's return to the boy who pretends to be Freddy Krueger so that he isn't afraid anymore. At least, that's what he thinks consciously. But underneath the surface, as research has shown, is an undercurrent of unconscious "wishful identification" with Freddy. Children, and even many teens, are usually oblivious to this type of influence.

Spheres of Influence for a Child's Growth with Mass Media Influences

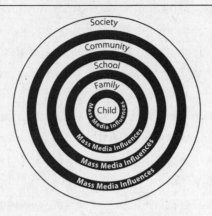

Mass media impacts the child within each sphere of influence. As the child grows, spheres of influence expand, making mass media effects pervasive and cumulative because they are amplified through relationships in each sphere of influence. The earlier a child develops a personal relationship with mass media, the more we can expect mass media's messages to impact the child's self-identity.

Once the external influences "get inside" of us, it can be confusing. We can't always identify an external influence as a "cause" of our actions. The two may have been directly related, but we may never connect them. The only thing we can do is to strive to be more conscious about what influences us to become the type of person we want to be. That means we must spend time in reflective thought. We have to "mind meander" to put influences in perspective. When kids are with screen technologies five to eight hours a day, they don't have enough time to be within themselves—to consider how violent images may be impacting them and their developing sense of self.

Mass media, by its very nature, focuses kids' attention on the external world. Take time to daydream? Who has time? Understand what you are saying to yourself? Why do that? Filling kids' lives with iPad apps and video games distracts them from self-reflection opportunities. When children are given time to go "inside themselves" without need of any external stimulation, they come to value their own thinking processes and capabilities in important ways. Too much time with externalized images on screens prevents children from knowing themselves. And they can't value what they don't know.

As youngsters grow into school-age children and school-age children mature into teens, the more time they spend with screen technologies, the more their lives are filled with violent images. They have little or no time to process these images and consider how the images are affecting them. If the research is true, very few parents are talking with their kids about the impact of media violence.

FROM IMITATION TO IDENTIFICATION: HOW MEDIA VIOLENCE IMPACTS SELF-IDENTITY

Let's look at how a steady diet of media violence—with images that are not adequately processed, either by the child alone or with a caring adult—affects children and teens at the following stages of development.

From Imitation to Identification:
How Media Violence Can Impact Self-Identity

Ages 3-5	Ages 6-10	Ages 11-14	Ages 15-18
Imitates cartoon violence	Sees violence as acceptable way to solve problems	Follows peers to inflict emotional or physical aggression	Identifies self as violent
Wants to be like violent characters	Sees violent characters as heroic	Thinks violence is "cool"	Thinks being violent is "normal"
Difficult to teach cooperative behavior	Sees self as a "problem" possibly as a "misfit"	Thinks and acts with harmful intent	Normalizes own violent behavior
Violent characters imbedded in imagination	Difficulty coming up with cooperative ways to get along with others	Surrounds self with like-minded peers	Justifies own violent behavior

Ages Three to Five

Learning is carried out in two stages: imitation and identification. As young children imitate the violence they see on screens through imitative play, they are learning to identify themselves as perpetrators of violence . . . from the very beginning of their lives! It has been found that the more unrealistic the character, the more preschoolers both want to be like that character and think they are like that character. Thus, odd, bizarre, and sensational violent outbursts on the screen capture their attention for mimicry in ways that the sedate, kind adults around them don't. Emotionally laden images are even more efficient at catching and holding the attention of youngsters than educational demonstrations. Because young children attend so readily to the visually exciting and emotional portion of the screen content, violent imagery impacts them profoundly. Since their cognitive abilities are limited, children are unable to put scary images into an understandable framework. Also, young children are unlikely to pick up on the subtlety of the images' mitigating information—such as negative motivations, punishment that occurs later in the program, or the suffering of victims—and put it into some kind of coherent, cause-and-effect context.

The impact of violent imagery on children is best understood within the context of normal child development. Children are born with an instinctive capacity and desire to imitate adult behaviors. That infants can, and do, imitate an array of adult facial expressions has been demonstrated in newborns as young as a few hours old—before they are even old enough to know that they themselves have facial features that correspond with those they are observing and imitating. Babies as young as fourteen months old clearly observe and incorporate behaviors seen on television. Dr. Brandon Centerwall makes a very important point when he observes in the documentary *Healthy Brain Development in a Media Age*, "Young children have an instinctive desire to imitate the behavior of others, but they do not possess an instinct for gauging whether a behavior *ought* to be imitated. They will imitate anything, including behaviors most adults would regard as destructive and antisocial." Since youngsters do not have the brain capacity yet for analysis, evaluation, or moral judgment, they are developmentally unable to discern the difference between fantasy and reality; if they did, we wouldn't have too many kids believing in Santa Claus or the tooth fairy. Therefore, they are incapable of interpreting violent images, of making personal sense out of them, without our help.

In the minds of young children, media violence is a source of entirely factual information regarding how the world works. Studies indicate that "real" to a young child appears to mean physically existing in the world. They may regard police dramas to be real because police officers do exist. One second-grade student in a study explained that the members of the Brady Bunch were real because "they have a refrigerator, and there are such things as refrigerators." And there is no limit to a child's credulity. For example, an Indiana school board had to issue an advisory stating that Teenage Mutant Ninja Turtles do not exist, because too many children had been crawling down storm drains looking for them.

When a young child sees somebody being shot, stabbed, raped, brutalized, degraded, or murdered on TV, to them it is as though it is actually happening. Imagine children of three, four, or five watching "splatter" movies in which they spend sixty minutes learning to relate to a cast of characters and then in the last sixty minutes of the movie they watch helplessly as their newfound friends are hunted down and brutally murdered. This is the moral and psychological equivalent of introducing a child to a group of new friends, letting him play with those friends, and then butchering them in front of him. And this happens to many children again and again throughout their early development.

While children experience cognitive confusion about what they see on the screen, that does not keep them from imitating violent behaviors. In fact, the more often children watch violent television programs and movies, the more likely it is that they will develop and sustain highly aggressive heroic fantasies for years to come. Then, in a vicious cycle, the children who create violent fantasy play and who identify with aggressive heroes are the ones most likely to be affected by media violence.

Writing in *Psychology Today* in 1975, the renowned cognitive psychologist Jerome Bruner first made the often-quoted observation: "Play is the serious business of childhood. . . . It is the vehicle of improvisation and combination, the first carrier of rule systems through which a world of cultural restraint replaces the operation of childish impulse." In the 1970s TV characters or movie heroes were only *a part* of a generative play experience—not the entire thing. Children incorporated the media images into original material such as reenacting an earlier trip to the grocery store or the anticipated vacation to the beach. Screen characters would be imitated within a context that included a broad range of real people from children's real-life activities. The child might be an action figure from TV one day, and then a postal worker he knew another day. A child would "try on" many adult roles—a gardener, a bus driver, a mom, an athlete, a teacher, dad, or film star. In becoming these real people, they would assume the inner dialogue of the person they became. "I love working in the garden" or "I am good at teaching kids." Experimenting with different ways of being, children explored within themselves different ways of becoming.

In children, by acting out people who do regular things and don't blow up or maim others for a living, a world of cultural restraint *could* replace the operation of childish impulse, as Bruner stated. By acting out play scenarios that mimicked emotionally and socially healthy adults, their imaginative play reinforced acceptable behaviors because the children used words to communicate with each other, not fists, as they expressed feelings, through language; not punches, as they negotiated differences, resolved conflicts, and solved problems using their ideas, not knee-jerk reactions. Play was as it should be: a process of learning and practicing pro-social roles.

Aggressive play is a normal part of a young child's experimentation. In fact, parents who refuse to buy toy guns for their youngsters report that guns will be made out of sticks, carrots, toilet rolls—basically anything children can get their hands on. One mother who had banned toy guns for her sons, ages two and four, found an old peanut butter and jelly sandwich they had shaped into a "toy gun" under her couch.

Children wanting to act out what they see on TV and in movies is entirely normal. What is not normal, however, is the almost exclusive acting out of violent roles over and over, so that the media-induced violent images become the sole source for the child's play fantasies. In his book *Play and Quality in Early Childhood: Educating Superheroes and Fairy Princesses*, Dr. C. Glenn Cupit, Senior Lecturer in Child Development in the School of Education at the University of South Australia, notes that "electronic media and their associated toys and artifacts provide predetermined scripts which many, if not all, children have learned and share, diminishing the need for . . . negotiations and the language and social skills involved in that process." The restrictive aspect of young children's play is currently a major concern of early childhood educators. Child-care providers often see the child who veers from the narrow script of a violent TV program ostracized by his or her peers or told to "play the right way"—meaning the way the violent TV or movie characters are behaving.

When children repeatedly imitate the violent behaviors they see on the screen, no social rules are being taught or reinforced. In fact, young children cannot possibly learn the social restraint Bruner referred to when their creative play consistently models the impulsive violent behavior they see on the screen. What Bruner didn't have to consider in 1975 was that young children who imitate anti-social or even deviant images can no longer be expected to absorb appropriate feeling states to learn social restraint and make healthy decisions in a social context. Rather, the child learns to push, shove, and kick. Hurting other people or dominating through force becomes an almost unconscious decision. Negative, antisocial images reinforce the young child's natural proclivities. Youngsters can't be expected to control their strong feelings—they must be taught to do that. And research has discovered that this can be done through superhero play only if the teachers or parents take time to involve themselves in the play and amplify prosocial messages. But if kids continually imitate antisocial, violent behavior in imaginative play scenarios without adult intervention, this not only makes it difficult to teach healthy alternatives, it traps children in the abyss of a repetitive, limited emotional repertoire. They become more and more distanced from their own abilities to make up prosocial images in their heads. It becomes harder for them to visualize other alternatives for problem solving except the violent behaviors they keep repeating in their play. As a result, they are not easily taught cooperative behaviors like sharing toys with peers or not shoving the child next to you in line.

The modeling of other children's cooperative behaviors and the teacher's instruction for "using words, not punches" fall short of the salient, sensational media images bombarding the child each day. Those are making the foremost impression on the fragile brain of youngsters in this age range—so much so that in their next stage of development, it can be difficult for adults to help them recognize and use nonviolent ways to solve problems. The youngster is on his way to seeing himself as an aggressive person. And by the teen years, it won't be easy to take back the cumulative impact of applauding violent behavior as a normal problem-solving technique and acceptable social norm throughout early childhood.

Ages Six to Ten

From violent cartoons to sensational, graphically violent movies, to horrifyingly violent video games—as our kids watch, they learn dialogue, behaviors, and attitudes that they absorb, scripts that turn up in their daily lives. Elementary-age girls average 5.5 hours a week, while elementary-age boys average 13 hours a week playing video games.

It's becoming a standard practice to introduce younger kids to violent video games—even if the games are clearly marked for teens or as "mature." Yes, it's fun to pretend to be a criminal whose adventures include bank robberies, assassinations, pimping, and street racing. But there is a cost. Nancy Guerro and L. Rowell Huesmann have demonstrated in their research that elementary school children's beliefs about aggression correlate with their aggressive behaviors. Like young children, kids at this age also need adult guidance to ensure that they don't mindlessly imitate people on the screen.

Video games, more than any other form of violent media, have the "unique ability to directly increase aggressive cognitions." They implant aggressive thinking into young brains, impacting key knowledge structures about self and the world. For instance, the child's understanding of personal power can certainly be affected, since playacting in violent video games means rehearsing deviant behaviors. Confusing a sense of personal agency with domination over others means that children can grow to feel powerful only when controlling or hurting others—a risky proposition at best.

Children ages six to ten need to develop a healthy sense of their own competency. In the words of noted psychologist Erik Erikson, this is the stage of "industry versus inferiority." Erikson posited the theory of psychosocial development with eight stages over the span of a lifetime. Each stage is characterized by a fundamental psychological conflict whose successful resolution allows progression to the next stage. For school-age kids, skill development and getting along with their peers comes to the forefront. Teachers, as well as coaches, take on important roles because they teach specific skills. Success in obtaining skills—whether academic skills like reading or writing, or other skills like sports abilities—means that the child feels success from his or her own initiative. Peer group approval, too, becomes a source of self-esteem. That may be an important reason why violent media is so popular—who wants to say no to one's peer group? It becomes challenging for parents to set limits on media consumption during this stage of development since the peer group has become important to the child for feelings of belonging. Smart parents replace violent video games with those requiring creativity and strategies so that children learn skills transferable to real-world situations. Teaching kids to choose alternative activities to violent entertainment reinforces their initiative; they begin to feel industrious, confident in their ability to achieve goals. Becoming competent to make healthy media choices at this age sets a positive trajectory for the rest of the child's life.

Elementary-school-age children can learn to act with intention within reason and limits. But with violent entertainment the intention is always to hurt, usually with no limits. Scripts form a "set of programs" inside the child's mind for solving social problems. Just like scripts guide an actor in what to do and say, these internal scripts are automated thinking that children will call upon to help them define situations and direct behaviors. They are more likely to act out in the classroom or at home than children who watch less violent media. And, unfortunately, with enough reprimands, they can come to think of themselves as "a problem"—as someone who has trouble fitting in with others.

Ages Eleven to Fourteen

"Maybe if we cut some of the more violent videogames, kids would be taught violence is wrong," wrote a middle schooler participating in the Challenge Program sponsored by the National Campaign to Stop Violence. The program gives middle school students an opportunity to examine the impact of violence by writing essays on the causes of and solutions for youth violence—an excellent way to help

We Construct Our Self-Identity from Both Internal and External Sources of Influence

Internal Sources

Conscious and Unconscious Thoughts and Feelings → Self-Identity ← Family, School, Community, Mass Media

External Sources

Self-identity is constructed from complex interactions of both internal and external sources of influences. But because we *experience* the external influences *as if* they were internal, and because so much brain processing is unconscious, we often do not or cannot separate the sources of influence within us. We often take into our self-identity influences that we don't question or challenge.

Copyright © 2013 Gloria DeGaetano. Used with permission.

kids reflect on how media violence might influence them. Without activities such as this, middle schoolers drift on a sea of violent entertainment, not understanding how it could affect their attitudes and worldview.

And it's a choppy sea. According to a 2010 study by the Kaiser Family Foundation, middle schoolers play video games more often than any other age group. They enjoy games with their friends, helping each other get new codes to learn how to play the games better. According to one study, 8 percent of middle schoolers reported playing video games six hours or more each day. Some begin to identify themselves as "gamers," a questionable role identity, potentially limiting their participation in other activities, such as reading or making music or learning a second language—activities that would broaden their experiences beyond violent entertainment, adding to their competence quotient.

Middle school kids also watch their fair share of TV and movies—on average twenty hours a week—seeing plenty of inappropriate content in the process. Physicians Iman Sharif and James Sargent examined the association between TV, movie, and video game exposure and school performance in middle school boys and girls. In a 2006 study they found that exposure to adult content in TV, movies, and video games had the "most consistent negative impact on school performance." Interestingly, they found that girls were more vulnerable if there were more cable movie channels in the home, whereas boys were more vulnerable if R-rated movie viewing was not restricted. When school performance suffers, so does the child's sense of self as a learner. Where is the child's attention when he or she watches TV, for instance? Not on schoolwork. Television programs and movies may not be telling children what to think, but they are very good at telling kids what to think about. Compelled by their significant findings, Sharif and Sargent recommended that "parents of middle schoolers limit weekday television and video game time to an hour or less a day and restrict access to adult media by limiting exposure to cable movie channels and R-rated movies and videos." This may seem like a radical move. Yet, without strict boundaries around adult content, violent images creep into kids' psyches, influencing how they will perceive themselves and how they will act toward others.

Often kids at this age are restless—not able to sit still with their own thoughts. They seek relief from boredom through their devices—games on their cell phones or tablets keep them occupied and "out of trouble." Breaking this habit would benefit kids tremendously. Discovering what they really want to do after being in that uncomfortable place within, kids discover different facets of themselves. They enrich their self-identity through initiation of new experiences. Watching TV or playing video games need not be the "go to" activity every time a child feels out of sorts. In fact, doing this only molds a self-identity that comes to recognize the self as dependent upon tech devices for feelings of satisfaction. If middle schoolers have been immersed in a steady diet of violent entertainment up to this point, it is very likely that by now they think "violence is cool" and surround themselves with peers who think likewise.

Middle school is a vulnerable time for both girls and boys. Boys may join peer groups to reinforce their idea of masculinity, even if that means they think being a man has to do with hurting others. Girls are strongly influenced by their self-perceptions. A 2001 classic study found that girls who hold a negative view of themselves and who believe peers view them negatively attempt to manipulate the social environment with the goal of punishing those who have wronged them and ensuring loyalty from those who might wrong them. This keeps them ever vigilant and often stressed and defensive with little self-confidence. In fact, other studies in 2001 and 2003 have shown that self-efficacy declines in girls during early adolescence. However, at age twelve boys are at risk too for poor self-identity because the research clearly shows that kids this age usually evaluate themselves in comparison to their peers instead of to absolute standards.

Ages Fifteen to Eighteen

As we have discussed, the research on desensitization shows that with increased familiarity with violent imagery comes more numbness. The cumulative effect of a daily media violence habit likely results in kids ready to defend virtual violence, unaware of its negative effects on their attitudes and values. They are much more likely to normalize antisocial, deviant depictions, since the horrific images don't linger or disturb teens after they have feasted at the table of violent entertainment all their lives.

The teen brain goes through a major overhaul. Brain science of the last two decades clearly demonstrates that brains "undergo a massive reorganization" between ages twelve and twenty-five with "extensive remodeling, resembling a network and wiring upgrade." Teens' typical rebellion, risk taking, and intent focus on peers are part of this process. Throughout it all, they "try on" different ways of being in the search for clarity about their own self-identity. Unfortunately, that may include acting out violent role models to the extreme.

Erikson referred to this stage as one of "identity versus role confusion." In this stage of psychosocial development teens question who they are, what is important to them, and what sort of person they want to be. While the teen can certainly explore these dimensions of self in the virtual world, immersing oneself in virtual reality at the expense of the real world stunts self-awareness and may be a sign of low self-esteem. In fact, adolescents with low self-esteem and high levels of rebelliousness or sensation seeking have increased media exposure.

A healthy adolescent self-identity is evidenced in increased autonomy, competence, and ability to relate well to others. Teens who accept responsibility for their decisions, who use thinking skills in ways that help them limit dangerous risks, and who enjoy preparing for their future indicate a well-adjusted concept of self. However, teens preoccupied with media violence are likely to experience relationship difficulties and be less motivated and less willing to think about their future. They may be caught in the web of lying to themselves about harming others, justifying the aggressive behavior that has become so much a part of their self-identity. Rather than enter adulthood with a strong sense of self and a capacity to stay true to who they are, teens culminate their violent media saturation back where they started. They enter their early adult years stuck in the same old patterns that they were in during childhood, not having learned to cooperate, negotiate, or restrain their "childish impulses."

Obviously, teen killers cannot easily restrain themselves. It's as if their own self-identity has become entangled with virtual fantasy. In many shooting sprees, for instance, the shooters put on a costume, like a trench coat, a hockey mask, or a military uniform—copying a video game character. These kids not only acted out the grisly scenarios from their favorite violent video games, but they also dressed up like their virtual world counterparts, as if to more closely identify with them. This enabled the shooters to "follow the script" they rehearsed daily in their video game play. The script goes like this: The perpetrator gathers up a bunch of guns and ammunition, goes to a place where there are a lot of people, kills as many people as possible, and then often kills himself. Most people could not carry out such a script. Our own sense of ourselves would absolutely not allow it. But kids who have been desensitized by lifelong exposure to violent media and trained to kill by first-person shooter games can easily come to see these horrendous acts as normative. Without a clear sense of who they are, they become someone else—someone who wants to harm others.

There is a common expression in brain research: "What gets fired, gets wired." Repetition of any activity fires the same brain pattern over and over again. This enables a quick response to situations without taking time for conscious evaluation. Athletes hone their skills by repeating the same moves, for example. A marksman gains accuracy with repetition. Frequently following aggressive scripts will affect the firing in our kids' brains, resulting in teens who not only identify with violent perpetrators but also consider their atrocious behavior normal, justifying it every step of the way.

What our kids tell themselves about themselves is the most important thing we need to know when they engage in violent entertainment. The younger the child, the more the sense of self is shaped by exposure to media violence. Let's provide counter scripts and role models that allow our kids—at every stage of their development—to construct stories about themselves as law-abiding, empathetic, socially competent, and emotionally intelligent individuals.

CHAPTER FIVE

ACTIONS SPEAK LOUDER
THAN WORDS

What we fail to do is often more serious than what we choose to do. To choose not to do something important is itself a choice that carries moral weight.

—Matthew Fox, *Sins of the Spirit, Blessings of the Flesh*

Y ou've probably had the experience with someone—on a volunteer board, in a corporate boardroom, or even with relatives around the kitchen table trying to plan a family reunion—who says, "Yes, I'll do it." And then nothing happens. Two weeks go by and, getting antsy, you ask the person for clarity. "Did you mean you will do such and such?" "Yes, of course, I'll get to it," he or she responds. So you wait, but again you hear nothing back. So for the next two weeks you send gentle reminders using phone calls, text messages, and Facebook postings, and finally the person responds. "Yes, I will get to it." But they never do. Incidents like this leave us feeling frustrated, angry, and even a little used. "Why agree to do something if you don't intend to do it?" you think. "Why assure me you want to help, but then never follow through?" It's crazy making. You have to move on, for your own sanity and to get anything productive accomplished, with reliable people who "walk their talk." We feel the same way about how the industry, government, and too many people handle the media violence issue. All talk, no action, while our kids, and our society, suffer the consequences. Don't be one of these people. There's too much at stake. And there's plenty to do.

We are both parents—five sons in total—so we know firsthand the incredible challenges of raising kids in a digital world. And we work with hundreds of parents and professionals each year who don't know how to tackle the issue in any meaningful way. That's certainly understandable. It's easy to feel overwhelmed by the size of the entertainment behemoth, the impact it has on children at all levels, and its obvious lack of restraint when it comes to using sensational violence.

But really, if we seriously intend to take action against media violence that will make a positive difference, we must become more comfortable with the understanding that yes, we are like salmon swimming upstream against the current—a strong one at that. And yes, it will take more individual energy, courage, and stamina than we may feel we have. And yes, it will mean consciously taking time to participate with others in schools and communities to weave collectively a protective safety net for our kids. In other words, it will take a lot from a lot of regular people.

This chapter discusses practical actions that will make significant, positive changes. The activities don't have to be time consuming. And you may be doing important things already, like helping children develop crucial protective factors. Remember, you don't have to do everything we suggest. Doing what you can means long-lasting effects for the children you know and love, and for the children of the future, as well.

ACTION AT HOME

If you haven't already, immediately put down this book and find out what video games your child plays. If you don't know the exact names, if you haven't at least played fifteen minutes of the game itself, if you haven't read reviews of the games, do so now. If you don't have a tracking system for knowing what your kids are doing online, begin that quest immediately by referring to the resources at the back of this book and looking at the options for Internet safety and app regulation. If your child is over at a friend's house right now or plans to be soon, find out what TV, movies, or video games he will play while there. If you don't know the parents of your child's best friends, plan a dinner right now to get acquainted with them so you all can be on the same page about the media your kids consume.

The number one best way to stop the harmful effects of media violence is through parental involvement—those "simple things" parents do every day are actually powerful change agents. Knowing exactly what video games kids play and what movies and TV programs they watch gives clout to our guidance and rules. We're in the know and our kids know it!

The suggestions below can further your quest to help your kids reduce exposure to violent programming and game playing. They give you practical tools that get down to the nitty-gritty of everyday life—collectively, call them a blueprint for action on the home front.

Use the "Four P" Framework

A big question is: How do we protect our kids and at the same time empower them to know what's going on? Or, put slightly differently, how do we protect their best interests without smothering them? Start by remembering the four P's:

- Process
- Perception
- Power
- Perspective

First, effectively addressing media violence as a family takes time. It's a *process* with all the highs and lows of an ongoing learning process—a few steps forward, a few back, then a few more forward again. Focus on progress toward reducing media violence as a risk in your child's life. And start where you are. If your kids have seen more than you would have liked them to, or if they are really hooked on violent video games, take action, knowing that steps you take now to remedy the situation can pay huge dividends in the long run.

If you are new parents and want to know how to get

started with your baby, begin by understanding that your ideal may not always be obtainable—we all run into stumbling blocks, and it's not the end of the world. We have heard colleagues who are child development specialists, doctors, psychologists, and media literacy professionals lament the amount of time their own children spend in front of the TV, or the way their kids are enamored of violent heroes. The point is, you can read all the pertinent studies, do everything you know to keep violent programming at bay, and have a wonderful, loving relationship with your kids, and they'll still probably go through phases that seem a little scary to you. So it's important to remind ourselves that we, as parents, are in it for the long haul. It's a process. What we do most consistently in that process is what matters most. The cumulative effects of our consistent attitudes, actions, and values educate and mold our kids, not a few isolated incidents they may encounter along the way.

Second, consider *perception*. How do your kids perceive your stance on media violence? Children, as we have demonstrated, imitate what they see and are very affected by their surroundings. And if they don't see and hear you condemning abject, graphic screen violence, they will not comprehend why it's bad for them. They're taking their cues from you, so make it clear that violence in all its forms is unacceptable. Very young children need to hear statements like these: "If people truly cared about children they wouldn't put that on for you to watch." "You are not old enough to understand that show, so we're not going to watch it. Let's see what else is on that will teach you good things." Older children and teens are hungry for your guidance and input, even though they take pains to act otherwise. Still, it's often hard to sit them down and discuss violent screen images without having them think you are cramping their style. But it can be done. Suggest watching movies at home together; compare older films with violence (*Patton, Ben Hur*, for example) to newer films and discuss the differences (there will be many!); chat about why certain kinds of entertainment are offensive and belittling to their audiences. And while you do all this, be very vocal about how you feel about sensational, graphic media violence. As we share our perceptions with our kids, we are imparting our values, what's most meaningful to us in raising them to be the people we want them to be. Consequently, they become more perceptive themselves, more capable of seeing through the lens of the values we have taught them.

Our third point has to do with *power*. How can we help our children feel powerful so they don't need to feed off the pseudopower of gruesome violent characters? Authentic power has nothing to do with physical force, domination, coercion, or inflicting suffering. As we help a child acquire a quiet, inner sense of self-confidence and self-respect, TV thugs or video game madmen become less glamorous and more inane. One self-possessed twelve-year-old boy couldn't see a reason for playing violent video games. "All you do is go around killing people, what's the fun in that?" he told his friends. His statement makes sense. Because he wasn't introduced to video game playing until he was eleven, this boy's self-identity was pretty solid before he started playing, so he didn't "buy into" the hype that violent video games were cool. He had a normal level of personal power for his age, so he chose the normal thing to do—bypass violent games in favor of mentally challenging educational games.

Video games aren't a necessity. In fact, the earlier they are introduced in a child's life, the more likely it is that the child will crave violent ones within a short time. Parents can make it so much easier on themselves by encouraging slower-paced computer games until the child's mental habits are set, usually somewhere around ages eleven to fourteen. The introduction of video games then will be less likely to lead to a reliance on "gaming for entertaining" and lessen the urge for violent video games as thrill-providing devices. And there are choices: If your child has a predilection for video games at a young age, we urge you to read up on and think about buying those games that do not contain gratuitous violence, those that challenge your child to think critically and creatively, and that require him or her to persevere at a mentally challenging problem. There are games that serve as jumping-off points for further study, hobbies, or educational pastimes, games that don't require marksmanship and an ability to shrug off carnage and killing. Take a look at the sources for nonviolent video games and family-friendly films in the resource section at the back of this book. These types of entertainment give kids healthy screen models for using personal power for good.

A lot of kids do possess a natural fascination with physical power, so why not steer them in a better direction by letting them practice a martial art? Many martial arts instructors are excellent role models for teaching power and knowing the right time and place to use it. Other parents

TOP TEN QUESTIONS TO ASK YOUR OLDER CHILD OR TEEN ABOUT MEDIA VIOLENCE

When asking these questions, expect debate, protest, resistance, shrugged shoulders, and silence . . . but keep asking these questions . . . be relentless. It's in the asking and discussing where all the learning is taking place, not in the answers.

1. If media and celebrities can influence you to buy things, why is it that media violence doesn't influence your attitudes and behaviors?

2. Just exactly what is cool about killing/hurting people? Please explain. I do not get this.

3. What are you thinking about when you walk away from that video game (movie, TV show)? What are you feeling when you play?

4. How is buying that violent video game (or movie) making you a better person?

have found that when their kids develop a talent in music or art, they are more self-reliant and less screen enamored. There are myriad ways we can build a child's confidence and sense of empowerment, and once that has been accomplished we're halfway there.

It's always a good idea to sit down with your kids and discuss the misuse of power in violent screen portrayals. As we've said, the worst kind of screen violence, the most reckless and irresponsible use of it, is when it is stylized and graphic, and there's no sense of a real aftermath to the action. Ask them why the perpetrator thinks that violence

5. If you had a little child, would you let him or her watch what you just watched? Why or why not?

6. What would your friends say to you if you told them you thought this violent video game (movie, TV show) was just plain stupid?

7. Write three sentences about what you learned from this violent movie (TV show, video game) and then answer this question: Do I like myself better or worse for watching (playing the video game)?

8. If you were the scriptwriter, how would you have reduced the gratuitous violence here and emphasized more the harsh consequences of violence?

9. Let's talk about some of the important distinctions between sensational portrayals and sensitive portrayals of media violence. Can you tell the differences?

10. Are you a victim of media manipulation? Why or why not? How do you know?

is the way to solve his problem. Young children may not be able to answer that question, but ask it anyway to get them thinking. Little ones also benefit from your asking these five questions as often as you can when you know they have seen violent images.

- Was this real or pretend? How do you know?
- What would happen to that man if he really hurt someone like that?
- How much do you think that punch (gunshot, stabbing, etc.) hurt that person?

- What would have been a better way to solve the problem than fighting (killing, etc.)?
- Did anything scare you? Let's talk about it.

Both children and teens need to be continually re-minded that those who are feeling small, afraid, weak, and helpless are often the first to resort to violence. And no matter how good it looks on-screen, how cool it makes the perpetrator seem, it's important for kids to understand the difference between domination over someone and control of a situation or event, and that a powerful person is one who knows you always have a choice—the choice to harm or the choice to help.

Finally, keep *perspective* on the situation. One divorced mother we know found out that her kids watched all kinds of violent fare every weekend when they spent time at their father's house. She was very concerned about the sit-uation and didn't know what to do. Our advice was simple. Start by doing what you can and then work from there. This woman was doing all the right things at her house and she did have custody of her children five out of seven days. The children were ages eight and ten when she began the ritual of inviting them to discuss what they watched on television at their dad's. The floodgates opened. They were consumed with what they took in on their weekend visits and knew it wasn't all good, clean fun. They were eager to talk about it. But like a lot of kids, they had no framework to discuss and understand what they saw. So when they re-turned from their father's, Mom asked them questions in a nonjudgmental way about what they watched. She listened carefully to them and affirmed their emotional reactions, explaining how camera angles, music, and quick-cut edits made violence seem more exciting. And she encouraged them to think about and question everything they saw. Her children are now well-adjusted young adults with keen insights into the human condition far beyond their years. The lesson here is: Don't overreact and keep open communication with your child or teen.

The Vital Five: The Top Protective Factors

The Vital Five are five essential needs of children—and adults—that often get shortchanged in our hectic, hurried, high-tech society. Distilled from the past two decades of brain research, consider these your daily guide to putting protective factors in place for your kids. The goal is to intentionally address as many of these five needs as you can throughout the day. It's a fun challenge. If you can't get to all of them every day, make the first one your focus and go from there.

1. *A Loving Parent–Child Bond*

Mobile devices encase children and parents in a peculiar world. Not exactly a world, but a portal to many worlds of countless possibilities—worlds that continually tempt us away from the world of the here and now, the world of the living, so to speak. Yet, if parents succumb too often, they become absent parents by default. Here, but not really. With their children, but not present *to* their children. If moms and dads are unapproachable, will children grow to seek validation from their machines, cementing an emotional bond with Siri while forgoing the messier relationships with parents altogether? We think that's a real possibility. Dr. Melissa Arca, a member of the American Academy of Pediatrics Council on Communication and Media, doesn't want that to happen. On her blog, *Dr. Mom*, she bluntly states, "All the connectedness in the world doesn't mean much to me if I'm disconnected to the ones I love."

Having fun together, talking often, and reading to and with our children builds our love bond with them. And in these activities kids hone important literacy skills as well. When you consider literacy, know that thinking and self-regulation skills develop in addition to reading and writing abilities. That's because literacy development grows the prefrontal cortex to enable higher-level reasoning and problem-solving abilities. Since the prefrontal cortex is an important component in dampening impulsive, aggressive behavior, children and teens with strong language abilities and problem-solving skills are more apt to be able to control themselves. That's good news, making literacy a significant protective factor against the harmful effects of media violence. So every time you spend time with your child connecting and communicating, you not only give her the gift of your loving presence, you also develop a powerful antidote for screen violence.

Literacy skills can actually help prevent violent behavior. Dr. Bruce Perry, the director of CIVITAS Child Trauma Programs at Baylor College of Medicine and Texas Children's Hospital, explains that "a striking example of the role of cognitive development (development of a literate population) on violence comes from historical accounts of violence. In the year 1340 in Amsterdam, the murder rate was in excess of 150 murders per 100,000 people. Two hundred years later the murder rate was below 5 per 100,000 people." We know that this deep drop in the murder rate could not be due to genetics. It is impossible for the genetics of a population to change that significantly in two hundred years. So, what changed in Amsterdam? Well, abundant research has shown that the development of higher-level cortical use of the brain plays a large and necessary role in controlling violent impulses. When people use their thinking brains, they are less likely to act out in rage. And that's what happened in Amsterdam, in fact all over Europe, after more people became literate. Dr. Perry points out that the "sociocultural phenomenon underlying the development of healthier and more capable cortices was, without question, literacy. The introduction of the printing press allowed the percentage of literate (i.e., cortically enriched, cognitively capable) individuals to dramatically increase. Over a few generations, the impact of a number of bright, abstract individuals transformed their society."

This is not to say that smart, literate people do not commit crimes, but they do commit fewer than people who are illiterate.

IT may sound like a simple solution—too simple to be believable—that literacy skills can act as a buffer to potentially violent behavior. But the more children are able to verbalize and think on higher levels, the easier it will be to teach them about consequences of violence. In addition, literacy skills give kids a profound edge in coming to terms with screen portrayals of violence. A rich vocabulary, along with know-how at self-expression, provide essential tools for articulating feelings, opinions, and ideas about media violence that a less literate child does not have. Plus, a literate child will be able to express loving feelings as you continue to enhance the bond between you as s/he grows.

2. An Interior Life

When kids complain, "I'm bored!" a typical reaction may be to turn on a screen so they can amuse themselves with a cool game or an interesting TV program or movie. Innocuous as this sounds, it could turn into a bad idea. By not allowing kids the discomfort of boredom, we take away a golden opportunity for them to figure out what they really want. One mother came to a doable solution after much frustration:

> When my sons, at ages seven and ten, would say to me, "We're bored," like most mothers I would give them my fabulous ideas: "How about writing that thank-you card to Grandma? What about a board game? Well, it looks like it's time to go outside," which they immediately rejected with upturned eyes and petulant mouths. They wanted their electronics and I would not cave in because they had already spent their two hours on them. One day, I found myself getting increasingly irritated as they countered

all my suggestions, but demanded [that I] figure it out for them. It finally dawned on me that as I was giving them ideas of things to do I was denying their ability to figure it out for themselves! So, I said to them, "I want you to sit on that couch over there and stay bored. Yes, that's right. Just sit there. When you are through being bored, you can get up." They looked at me like I was nuts and then looked at each other, as they had no alternative but to do as I said. They knew from the tone of my voice that I was fed up. After sitting for a while and "just thinking" their eyes lit up and they jumped off the couch to play an original game they wanted to try out. Without this opportunity to think things through in self-reflection, I doubt if they would have come up with the game. From then on, we issued "think-time-outs." This really helped me (and them!) not make an app or their video games the "go to rescue remedy" as much.

Whether it's through "think-time-outs" or asking kids questions so they have to muse within, whenever we direct their focus inside of themselves, we help them grow an interior life. The startling ease with which screen machines keep children quiet, yet distracted from their internal voice, means that parents today have to be more intentional than ever to make sure their kids spend some time within themselves. Like the human need for bonding with loving parents that enables future healthy relationships, "going inside" regularly enables the child or teen to bond with self—thus developing the necessary foundation for a healthy self-identity. After all, sorting and sifting through inner ideas and feelings builds self-knowledge and important self-understandings for tackling life's challenges.

3. *Image Making*

Kids in a mass media world are inundated with images not of their own making. They don't see their own images when they watch TV or a film or play a video game. They don't make up these images in their own head. All the images are given to them. Alarmed, teachers report that when they read aloud to children in their classrooms, some children say they don't "see pictures in their heads" of the characters in the book. Without opportunities to be in their own imaginations when consuming screen images four to six hours daily, kids don't get much practice using their imaginations.

A direct way to give children practice in image making is *listening* to stories, rather than watching them. Just as reading to our kids can help them process stories, so can using audiobooks for those times when we are too busy or too stressed to take time out to read.

There are many terrific audio selections available these days in libraries and on the Internet. Kids' lives are enriched in many ways by listening to a wide range of audio input. Even teens can enjoy listening to classics such as old radio shows like *The Shadow* or the original *Superman* series.

As children and teens hear and read language without accompanying pictures, they must make up the pictures in their own minds. With younger children we may read a beautifully illustrated book and there may be twenty or so pictures. And that's okay because there's still no picture for everything in the book, as is the case with TV programs or movies, or when playing a favorite video, computer, or app game. When reading books, watch out for the "pop-ups" in eBooks for young children. These continual interruptions that attract children's attention to a picture could interfere with their thought process and distract from their own image making. But whether on paper or on a screen, or through audio input, a daily family practice of discussing narratives goes a long way toward helping children develop both sequential thinking patterns and metaphoric abilities for imaginative thought—and that process builds resiliency against the harmful effects of violent imagery. This simple practice can yield big results.

4. Creative Expression

If screen time dominates kids' leisure time, what are they actually creating? Without other pastimes, like playing a musical instrument or learning a foreign language, kids aren't fully living life outside of screens. Yet, when watching TV, they're not making up anything of their own. When they're playing video games, they enter the world of someone else's creativity, not their own.

Too many kids these days could easily come to distrust their own creative capacities simply because they have not had enough experience using them. Commonplace forms of creativity, like stamp collecting, crafts, or sewing, open up new worlds and help kids develop their unique talents. Bring back a family game night—board games, that is—or have fun teaching the kids card games. Doing something new and different brings parents and children a sense of aliveness and connection to life and to each other. With regular opportunities for creative expression kids learn to value themselves as capable creators. They tap into their intrinsic motivation, making it easier for them to know their own talents. Going beyond present limitations to generate something better, creative expression provides the necessary foundation to become a social innovator. Kids learn that thinking and acting "out of the box" can be fun and they can effect change—often yielding extraordinary results for themselves and others.

5. *Contribution to Others*

By contributing to others, children and teens grow up learning their self-worth. They wish to give to others, and then eventually to the greater good. We may say to ourselves, "He will be on the iPad only while I push him in the cart down the grocery aisles." But this four-year-old with eyes fixated on the small screen that she holds in her hands isn't helping Dad pick out the freshest peaches; isn't involved in figuring out what will go with the hamburgers for tonight's dinner; and has no interest in thinking about what Grandma will like to eat when she comes for a visit. Not including the child in conversation about these decisions misses an important opportunity to help her feel like she belongs to the family. On this grocery trip, the girl learned that what's most important is playing the game on her iPad, not talking to her dad, not thinking about or anticipating the needs of her family, or how she could contribute to them.

We can reframe chores as opportunities for our kids to contribute to the good of the family, partly to train them to contribute later in life to the common good of a larger community. In discussing with kids why they must feed the cat or take the dog for a walk or empty the dishwasher every day, in addition to giving them the regular spiel about learning responsibility, we can explain to them that they are an important part of the family and that their contribution is valued and needed. Our children begin, then, to see their small part as integral to the smooth working of the family. As they learn authentic participation within the family, they also acquire the motivation to contribute to life beyond the family. Taking time to work at a soup kitchen feeding the hungry or visiting a senior care facility teaches powerful lessons about compassionate contribution to others. For service outside of the home to be personally meaningful, though, kids must first learn about contribution as relationship. That's best done by contributing to those they love and relate to each day. We tap into our children's need for belonging whenever we encourage them to contribute, no matter how small the act. They learn about purpose and meaning in their lives. They feel needed—because they belong. It's much better for them to feel they belong to us than to a virtual community of violent video game players.

These five vital developmental needs are summarized in the Vital Five chart, along with the important cognitive emotional, social, and moral developmental lessons learned when they are met. The Vital Five grow deep abilities and critical skills that enrich children's lives, often through

The Vital Five™: Daily Protective Factors

	Parent-Child Bond	Interior Life	Image Making	Creative Expression	Contribution
Cognitive	▪ Organized thought ▪ Reasoning processes	▪ Introspection ▪ Mental models	▪ Plan & strategize ▪ Problem solving	▪ Generative thinker ▪ Originality	▪ Synthesis ▪ Systems thinking
Emotional	▪ Capacity for intimacy ▪ Affective expression	▪ Self-determination ▪ Self-discipline	▪ Envision possible ▪ Stress Reduction	▪ Intrinsic motivation ▪ Knows own strengths	▪ Belonging ▪ Resilience
Social	▪ Trust self & others ▪ Self-regulation	▪ Restraint ▪ Honest curiosity	▪ Learn from experience ▪ Leadership capacities	▪ Social innovator ▪ Honors others' viewpoints	▪ Respects interrelatedness ▪ Celebrates diversity
Moral	▪ Loves self & others ▪ Cooperative	▪ Has a conscience ▪ Knows own values	▪ Empathy/compassion ▪ Life purpose	▪ Values others' creations ▪ Appreciates beauty	▪ Meaning beyond self ▪ Values social justice

seemingly "little things" parents do each day. For instance, when we're having a good time hiking with our family on a sunny day, we aren't usually thinking about how this family bonding time prepares our kids for healthy intimacy with others or how our child is learning to trust others or regulate his own behavior—we're just having a good time with our kids. When parents focus on these five crucial human needs, children and teens learn many important lessons that serve as protective factors for resisting the harmful effects of violent entertainment.

Family Media Literacy

Research consistently demonstrates that media literacy empowers kids to deconstruct and understand screen images, giving them analytic abilities that help them keep from succumbing to the harmful effects of media violence. With any family media literacy activity, it's important to remember that children of various ages and stages of development need slightly different rules and guidelines. The younger the child, the more important it is to protect him or her against all forms of violence in entertainment. As children develop literacy skills, higher-level thinking abilities, and more self-monitoring and self-calming capabilities, they are better equipped to discuss violent imagery, understand its impact, and, ultimately, deal with it more effectively. This is what we think all parents want for their children—the ability to respond thoughtfully to images of violence. And for that to happen, it means we have to become very involved, right from the beginning.

The media literacy activities listed in the resources section can get you started with thought-provoking discussion about screen violence for different age groups: ages three to five, six to ten, eleven to fourteen, and fifteen to eighteen.

As you make discussions about screen violence a part of your family's routine, keep in mind these two basic principles:

Establish a Few Rules and Strive for Consistency

Until the entertainment industry "gets it," either by legislative force, parental pressure, or some epiphany on their part, it's basically up to us to set boundaries for our children concerning violent entertainment. The average American child watches four hours of television each day through the most formative years, until age eighteen. So let's start here, by decreasing the amount of time your child spends in front of the television. Remember that, as we discussed in chapter 2, greater screen time is correlated with higher levels of aggression and lower school performance. There's even a growing body of research to indicate time spent with video games and with TV reduces kids' attention span in the classroom.

We realize that reducing the amount of viewing time is perhaps the toughest part of this equation, but you'll get results. Moderate viewers who watch one or two hours of television a day are much more likely to have other areas of interest and be more successful in school than are heavy viewers. So the bottom line, as advised by the American Academy of Pediatrics, is to reduce all screen time (including TV, computers, digital devices, and video games) to one or two hours a day. There are families that are adopting a "no television" policy with their children and getting good results. Although this is not a viable solution for many parents, and we're not saying that television is completely devoid of good programming for children, completely cutting television out of a child's diet is working for some.

A worthy goal is to cut back weekly time spent for all screens. Here are some ways to do this:

- Ensure that kids finish their homework before they watch television or play a video game; use a timer to indicate when screen time must end.
- Create a "budget" of ten hours of screen time weekly—and enforce it. One way to do this is to provide "time coupons," ten thirty-minute coupons for younger children or ten one-hour coupons for older kids. Give the coupons to them at the beginning of the week and let them choose how and when they will "redeem" the coupons. This is an excellent way to teach them control and choice making, as they will quickly have to decide how to spend their allotted screen time each week.
- Make time on the weekend to sit down as a family and figure out what the kids will watch during the upcoming week.
- Let the kids make decisions about what DVDs and TV programs they will watch, or video games they will play, based on choices that you offer them. Getting them involved in the process of choosing when and what they will watch reinforces healthy TV and

video habits. And children learn your values and how to incorporate them in their daily decision making.

• As kids get older, let them earn greater viewing time when they demonstrate control and wise choices.

It's especially important to note that if a child is experiencing difficulties such as behavior or learning problems or hyperactivity, overuse of TV and video games usually exacerbates the problem, taxing parental patience and adding to the child's stress. In cases such as these, the less screen time the better.

Another area that parents can concentrate on is the physical placement in the home of the television set and/or computer. We strongly suggest that parents follow the recommendation of the American Academy of Pediatrics to not allow television sets in their children's bedrooms. We think the same when it comes to computers. Of course, there are exceptions, especially with computers, as their use pertains to learning and homework, but it really is best in most cases to avoid having younger children in front of either device without some kind of supervision. Often families find success with putting the laptop or computer a child uses for homework in a community area so their online time is monitored.

Address Peer Pressure Directly

Peer pressure has been an excuse for kids since the beginning of time. We wouldn't let our kids buy guns if they said everyone had one; we wouldn't let them deal drugs because their friends did; and we wouldn't let them jump off the Brooklyn Bridge even if it was all the rage. So we absolutely should not let down our guard when it comes to watching and playing graphically violent fare. Abstaining won't kill our kids, or anyone else.

Peer pressure is perhaps our biggest stumbling block to getting kids on the right track, and this is true with almost everything bad for them. One new father we know feared that his efforts to keep his child away from video games and on-screen violence would result in the boy being an outcast with his classmates. You'd be surprised at how little peer pressure really matters with children before puberty.

Children are extremely adaptable. If we take a stand in our homes, children respect that we "walk our own talk." The "everyone else gets to watch it" or "everyone else plays those games" arguments can be countered by explaining that in your home you do things certain ways for certain reasons. Your child may resist at first, but many parents we know have found that to their surprise, the kids give up the battle to be "like everyone else" and acquiesce to their parents' standards when they are encouraged to be "like themselves."

The developmental tasks during childhood revolve around building a strong self-identity and social skills. If children are excluded from social interactions because they're not familiar with the latest app, TV program, movie, or video game, their world does not collapse. They don't lose face. In fact, they usually learn valuable lessons and gain the respect of their peer group.

What parents need is to focus not so much on whether the child is missing out on a culturally induced childhood

"necessity," but rather on building the child's sense of identity and resiliency. If all parents started addressing this
problem, our kids wouldn't have nearly as much problem
with peer pressure. Peer groups would take their cues
about what's important from parental values, not from
hawkers of violent media.

Take special care with young teens. From about ages
eleven to sixteen, kids want to be like their peers and
around their peers as much as possible. Parental influence
takes a backseat, at least on the surface. By developing a
strong sense of self in the early years, by not caving in to
peer pressure during those formative years, teens now have
the wherewithal to observe their strong, normal desire to
like their friends and then make good decisions about what
is right for them in the end. What we have instilled up to
this point in a child's life almost seems to go underground,
fermenting somewhere in the depths, but not clearly visible.
Have a look at the advertising of certain violent films, TV
shows, and, especially, video games, and you'll see that it ze-
roes right in on this age group's isolation, rebelliousness, and
sense of powerlessness. But know that everything you did
in the early years is there, brewing within your child. The
more you trust it, the more your child will, too.

Picking our battles around peer pressure at this age
means making compromises so that you continue to teach
your teen your values: "I won't let you go see that movie
with your friends, but remember, I am letting you stay
overnight at Pete's tomorrow night." "No, I won't give you a
subscription to Netflix, but I did buy you that CD I wasn't
so crazy about." "As I keep telling you, I won't buy violent

video games, but I will upgrade your system so you can get better sports games." If we link the "no" with a "yes," chances are their arguments will be shorter and we will win the important battles. And remember an important tenet in parenting well: A "no" is really a "yes." When we tell our kids "no," we are actually saying "yes" to what matters most to us and what we want to matter to them.

We hope you understand that there are no hard-and-fast rules here. Media literacy in the home is part intentional and part incidental, a matter of capturing the educational moments as they come up in the day-to-day and keeping our eye ever on the goal: an enlightened, intelligent, and loved child—our best defense against the harmful effects of media violence.

ACTION IN OUR SCHOOLS AND COMMUNITIES

Moving from the home front, let's have a look at key actions to take in our schools and communities.

Media Literacy Education

A lot of schools require kindergartners to use an iPad or give older kids regular homework that requires Internet access but don't have a media literacy curriculum in place. Teaching media literacy in our schools is paramount if we want our children to be responsible users of screen technologies as adults. Combining media literacy education with helping kids control their media exposure is the best way to be effective. The Stanford Medical School SMART

Curriculum demonstrated that turning media off, even for
as little as ten days, reduced third and fourth graders' ag
gression and bullying. A website has been developed by a
group of educators that offers free media literacy activities, pre-K through grade 12, for both teachers and parents,
along with guidelines for kids to participate in a screen
"detox." Based on Stanford's SMART Curriculum, www
.TakeTheChallengeNow.net holds much promise for teaching kids self-awareness and self-restraint.

Parents also can be influential in helping schools get
started on media literacy. One mom we know got fed up
when her daughter came home and wanted to use Google
to find something for her homework assignment. Since
her daughter was six years old at the time, she was outraged. After a visit with the principal, she found out that
the school did have a safeguard within their computer system when kids used search engines. Whew! But then that
brought up another topic for discussion. If the schools had
safeguards, but the kids came home expecting to use the
search engines and the parents were unaware that the kids
were using the search engines . . . well, you see where this
could lead. The school got the point. Because of this one
mother's leadership, the school decided to help parents
learn more about what they could do in regard to Internet safety at home. But that was just the first step. The
principal and teachers soon saw the need for a comprehensive curriculum in media literacy for all children in grades
K through 12, which could integrate well with social studies and English classes. If we want kids to be savvy users
of screen technologies, we need to do much more than

teach them the mechanics of using computers and digital devices—we must teach them to be purposeful and discerning when they do so. In another school a mom took the initiative with her PTA to begin an ongoing discussion about Internet safety with her Facebook community of parents, sharing information on that topic as well as educational apps for kids, and discussing what they all could do to help their kids self-manage their electronics and their access to inappropriate content, including media violence.

Be an Intentional Influence

We can bring up media violence and its role as a significant factor impacting youth aggression every chance we get. Individuals in all walks of life, from judges to doctors to social workers, can begin to take effective action once they understand the role of screen violence in fostering violent activity. For example, a juvenile court judge in Florida, after hearing the facts on this issue, is now including in his sentencing such things as community service at animal control centers, humane societies, and hospices to give youthful offenders some personal experience of death; removal of all point-and-shoot games from the home—and prohibition from being in the presence of these at friends' homes, malls, and so forth; and no viewing of R-rated media. We educate the public at large when we dare to include media violence as part of the equation anytime we are in a position to help children or youth. And we can do so using many of the hats we wear as we raise our kids. For instance, we can speak up at a PTA meeting and begin an ongoing discussion group—even if only a few people join us! We can train babysitters on alternative activities for young children so they are informed about reducing youngsters' exposure to media violence. We can lead a discussion of these issues with young people in our places of worship or community organizations. If we are members of our local business community, we can form alliances to get the word out about the harmful effects of violent video games. By consciously looking for ways to influence our community, we will start seeing the many opportunities around us.

Pressure Others to Do Something

The first response by many in the violent entertainment industry when confronted with allegations of negligence is invariably "It's the parents' responsibility to keep an eye on what their kids watch and play with." Yes, it is the parents' responsibility. But it is also the parents' responsibility to protect their kids from guns, tobacco, alcohol, pornography, drugs, and explosives. And in all of these areas the community at large helps parents in their struggle. Our society has deemed that marketing and selling .44 Magnums, cigarettes, booze, X-rated films and literature, cocaine, and dynamite to children is illegal. Knowing this, and faced with what we've demonstrated in this book, we must ask why, in this one vital area of violent entertainment, parents should be left on their own.

"We wouldn't sell it if people didn't buy it" is a favorite response. But this is pimp logic; drug dealer logic. Except that even pimps and drug dealers generally won't try to market to small children, and they don't claim a constitutional right to sell their products to our kids. Surely an industry that markets products to children can be held to a higher moral standard than this. There are two effective ways to accomplish this.

1. *We can educate parents on a national level.* Given that there are campaigns to convince Americans to "buckle up," or warn us against the dangers of drunk driving, yet none to inform parents of the potential harm associated with exposing kids to media violence, we must create one through grassroots efforts. We've made some headway in the last few years, but there are just too many parents who are still completely uninformed about the issue. Schools could make sure that their newsletters contain vital research information like what we have put in this book. PTAs, school boards, and administrators could make it a priority for kids to learn about the harmful effects of media violence and be encouraged to discuss the issues with their parents. A few vocal leaders in a community, such as Girl Scout and Boy Scout leaders, coaches, and church groups, could inform hundreds of parents. More informed parents mean more potential pressure on the entertainment industry—and fewer sales of violent DVDs and video games.

2. *We can put pressure on the violent entertainment industry to change their tactics.* Even the tobacco and alcohol industries accept the need for warning labels on their products, and it is time for the TV, movie,

and video game industries to at least meet this moral standard. The existing ratings systems and warnings, when there are warnings, are not enough. They are also not that truthful. Putting pressure on the industry to make the warnings accurate would be an important achievement, even though violent video games and movies are easily now downloadable. An accurate ratings system sends a message to our kids that society doesn't condone certain types of violent entertainment for children and teens.

E-mail campaigns can be effective. Send opinion pieces and letters of complaint en masse, voicing your joint concerns and demanding changes. In one evening, around a social event, a group could each send messages to the presidents and CEOs of entertainment companies, alerting them that there are concerned citizens out there who find on-screen violence marketed and sold to children offensive and wrong. At the same time, with the same keystroke, a copy of this message could be sent to senators and representatives at both the state and federal levels. This would educate legislators about the will of their constituents. Such action, multiplied on a national level, could mean several million e-mail messages received by the leaders of the entertainment industry in America, who would then only be lying to themselves when they claimed they were giving the people what they wanted. Several million e-mail messages to legislators would give them the backing to stand up to the special interest groups.

Social media is another powerful way of gaining visibility about the issues. Gathering like-minded people with a common vision through Facebook, Twitter, personal blogs, and other forms of social media can help local communities work with others on a national level. Join us on the Facebook page for this book (https://www.facebook.com/Stopteaching ourkidstokill) if you would like to participate in collective action against media violence.

Lobby for Legislation to Protect Kids

It has been said that the law is the best teacher. This means, for example, that the ultimate purpose of seat-belt laws is to inform citizens about something that is important to all of us. The possibility of getting a ticket is not what makes most people buckle up their kids; they do it because they love their kids and they want to protect them. But the existence of seat-belt laws serves as a powerful means to educate citizens about their responsibilities, not only to warn them of the dangers of not wearing seat belts. The very existence of the law shows that our whole society says this is the right thing to do. Similar legislation in the realm of screen violence can have the same effect. Unfortunately, when states try to put some restrictions on kids' access to gruesome media violence they don't succeed.

In 2005 California passed a state law that imposed a civil fine of up to $1,000 on any person who sells or rents a violent video game to a person under the age of eighteen. They defined a violent video game as a game in which you "kill, maim, dismember, or sexually assault an image of a

human being," and one that a "reasonable person, considering the game as a whole, would find . . . appeals to a devi
ant or morbid interest of minors" and "is patently offensive
to prevailing standards in the community as to what is
suitable for minors."

The video game industry fought all the way to the U.S.
Supreme Court to overturn this law. The opposing sides
both presented briefs to the Court. The first brief was written by a group of thirteen experts in the field of media violence and signed by 102 other scholars and scientists, making
a clear statement about the harmful effects of media violence and violent video games on children. The other brief
was from a group of individuals gathered by the video game
industry. To this day it is unclear who wrote the document,
but it was signed by eighty-two individuals, a large number
of whom were video game industry representatives.

A powerful document was prepared comparing the
credibility and qualification of the authors of these two
briefs. In this document it was revealed that the number of
articles on the harmful effects of media violence published
in leading, peer-reviewed journals was 338 times greater
than the number of articles in which these effects were
denied. Indeed, only 13 percent of the video game industry reps who had authored the Supreme Court brief had
written so much as a single article on media violence. But
all the scientific evidence didn't matter. On June 27, 2011,
Justice Antonin Scalia, reading the 5 to 4 majority opinion in *Brown v. Entertainment Merchants Association*, said
video games were protected by the First Amendment. And
that was that.

When California enacted its law, a Federal Trade Commission (FTC) study had found that nearly 70 percent of unaccompanied thirteen- to sixteen-year-olds were able to buy M-rated video games. But as of the FTC's most recent update to Congress, 20 percent of those under seventeen are still able to buy M-rated video games, and breaking down sales by store, one finds that this number rises to nearly 50 percent in the case of one large national chain. And the industry could easily revert to the substantial noncompliance that existed in 2004, particularly after this broad ruling reduced the industry's incentive to police itself.

We shouldn't be content with "self-regulation" and "voluntary restraints" for the violent entertainment industry, just as we do not allow the alcohol, tobacco, gun, drug, or pornography industries to voluntarily make up the rules. No, they are forced by legal means to keep our kids safe. The same should hold for the violent entertainment industry. We urge you to consider gratuitous, sensational media violence just as detrimental as the other products banned to children. Make waves. Disturb the system. Call or write to your federal and state representatives explaining why laws are needed to make the entertainment industry more accountable. And remember, legislation will come more quickly if you make your voice heard. Let the manufacturers and distributors know how you feel. Above all refuse to buy violent video games. When enough people stop purchasing these murder simulators, and the industry feels the financial effects, they will sit up and notice, since children and teens make up a big part of their market. And that will be a good beginning.

YOUR ACTIONS SPEAK MUCH
LOUDER THAN THEIR WORDS

When the first edition of this book was published in April 1999, the tragic events at Littleton had just occurred and President Bill Clinton made it a priority to address the issue. He called for the FTC and the Justice Department to look at whether the makers of violent television, movies, and video games were "improperly marketing this violence to children." In the first edition, we called this action "a solid step forward." But we were naive back then. We believed our leaders meant what they said—that their words would be followed by effective action.

In fact, over the last fifteen years, very little has been accomplished. Media violence has grown more horrific and pervasive. Antisocial, deviant entertainment continues to be marketed and sold to children and teens. Too many parents show a disturbingly complacent attitude toward their children's consumption of media violence.

We are now at a critical crossroads, and so much of our children's future depends on what we do, or don't do, today. We have our marching orders: It is time for the people to lead. We cannot wait for legislatures to act. We cannot wait for judicial systems. And we certainly cannot wait for the entertainment industry to change course. Our kids deserve more than talk. It's time for action. Let's trust that the actions each of us takes will make important changes, because they will.

RESOURCES

A DEFINITION OF HARMFUL MEDIA VIOLENCE

The following is a definition of harmful media violence, distilled from the scientific evidence. Let it act as a useful lens for viewing any type of entertainment or playing the hundreds of video games on the market.

Violence is the intentional use of force to harm a human being or animal. Its outcome is injury—physical or psychological, fatal or nonfatal. It is true that violence is a part of the real world. However, we do not take our children to see autopsies performed as entertainment, nor do we invite someone into our living room to kill, brutally beat, or rape another person for our children to witness for their amusement.

Therefore, portrayals of violence in the media that glamorize and/or sensationalize violent acts toward other human beings or animals and show them as acceptable behavior provide a socially aberrant environment in which it is difficult to raise emotionally healthy children. Also, the prevalence of violence on television, in movies, and video games in itself imparts an implicit acceptability to the vicarious experience of violence and pushes the boundaries of cultural norms into the realm of social deviancy. A synthesis of the research shows that harmful media violence includes the following:

- Plots that are driven by quick-cut scenes of gratuitous violent acts delivered with rapid-fire frequency using graphic, salient technical effects.
- Graphic, sadistic revenge, torture techniques, inhumane treatment of others in a context of humor, trivialization, glibness, and/or raucous "fun."
- Explicitly depicted violent acts shown through special effects, camera angles, background music, or lighting to be glamorous, heroic, "cool," and worthy of imitation.
- Depictions of people holding personal and social power primarily because they are using weapons, or using their bodies as weapons, and dominating other people through the threat of violence or through actual violence.
- Gratuitous, graphic, gory, detailed violent acts whose intent is to shock.
- Violent acts shown as an acceptable way to solve problems or presented as the primary or only problem-solving approach.
- News programs that explicitly detail murder and rape, with information and graphic images not necessary for understanding the central message.

It should be noted, however, that any form of aggression on the screen has the potential to make children more aggressive. The more graphic and horrific the violence, the more likely the negative effects. Research clearly demonstrates that sensational media violence causes children and teens to become more aggressive and mean, creating fear, a lack of sensitivity to all forms of violence, and an increased appetite for violence—in real life and on the screen. An early preference for violent programming is a strong predictor of aggressive and antisocial behavior as an adult. Is the child or teen identifying with the perpetrator or the victim? Sensational portrayals offer children a justification for violent acts in real life and perpetuate socially dangerous attitudes, behaviors, and values. On the other hand, sensitive portrayals of violence can promote empathy and compassion because they depict real-life suffering and its consequences. Such portrayals can evoke understanding of the human condition because in no way do they suggest that the suffering, murder, and mayhem is fun.

MEDIA LITERACY ACTIVITIES TO
COUNTER MEDIA VIOLENCE

Please note: The age levels are suggestions only. You can adapt any of these activities for a child or teen of any age.

AGES THREE TO FIVE

Talk about real-life consequences.

If the screen violence were happening in real life, how would the victim feel? In real life what would happen to the perpetrator of the violence? Compare what's on the screen to the consequences of what happens when someone hurts another person in the real world.

Violence is not the way to solve problems.

Emphasize that hurting another person in any way or destroying property is wrong and won't solve a person's problems. Choose a problem your child encountered recently, such as another child taking a toy away, and talk about the reasonable way the problem was resolved or could have been resolved—without hurting anyone.

Anger is natural.

Talk about the fact that we all get angry, that it's normal. It's what we do with our anger—how we cope with it and express it—that's important. When screen characters hurt people out of anger, it's because they have not learned how to deal with their anger.

Your child could make a list of screen characters who know how to deal with their anger in positive ways.

Count the number of violent acts.

While watching a favorite cartoon with your child, count the number of actual violent actions. Point out that these are harmful to others and you would never allow her to do such things to others. Total the number of violent actions at the end of the program and ask your child if she thought there were that many. Decide not to watch cartoons or any shows with such violent actions.

Talk about real and pretend.

If your child is exposed to a violent movie or video game, it is especially important to talk with him about the fact that the images were pretend—like when your child plays pretend—and that no one was actually hurt. Make it a common practice to talk about the differences between real and pretend with any TV programs or movies your child watches. Understanding this concept is basic to becoming media literate!

AGES SIX TO TEN

Get specific.

Ask your child: "What type of violence do you see most in your favorite shows, movies, or video games?" Then encourage her to keep a record of how many of the following acts are viewed in a week: threat with a weapon, unwanted sexual advances, rape, murder, slap or punch, fistfight, someone run over or hit by a car, knife wound, gun wound, property destroyed. Discuss with your child what she has learned about screen violence.

Picture a world without media violence.

Have your child imagine that violence was suddenly eradicated from all television, movies, and video games. Discuss such questions as: "What would take its place?" "What would you miss?" "What would the general population think about the eradication of media violence?" "Would the absence of media violence have any effect on real-life violence?"

Make a plot line of a favorite show or movie.

When watching an action TV program or movie, ask your child to write down the introduction; the problem; the search for the solution; the solution; and the ending. After the show ask your child to consider if the violence was really necessary to the plot. Other questions to ask might be: "Is violence shown as a solution?" "Could there have been an equally effective ending without the violence? Why or why not?"

Rewrite violent scripts.

In this activity your child acts as a screenwriter or video game designer and uses his creative ideas to change the violent script of a program or video game to a nonviolent one.

The goal is to eliminate the violence and come up with alternative solutions to the problems. Depending on the child's maturity and skills, this activity can involve drawing pictures rather than writing. Or the writing could consist of an outline. Encourage your child to pay special attention to those elements that must be changed in order to eliminate the violence: Is it the people, the places, the time, the situation? Discuss your child's story with him and point out changes from the original.

Make up a different hero.

Choose a favorite TV program or movie—one that your child is familiar with and enjoys watching—that contains some violence. An action cartoon works well for this activity.

Before the show begins hold a conversation with your child and say something like this: "As you are watching today, I want you to imagine another character being in the show (or cartoon)—someone you make up from your own imagination. This person can be male or female, tall or short, young or old. The only thing you have to make sure of is that this person solves all his or her problems through talking, cooperation, and negotiation. Never through hurting anyone or destroying property." Once the character has been chosen, ask your child to describe him or her in detail and how this imagined character (IC) might act in various situations. Then watch the program or cartoon and while watching, ask such questions as: "What is your IC doing now?" "What makes your IC strong? Smart? Creative?" "How would your IC solve the problem?" "What does your IC want to tell you about this show?"

AGES ELEVEN TO FOURTEEN

Discuss sensational versus sensitive portrayals.

In a discussion with your young teen about media violence ask such questions as: "When a violent act occurs on the screen, how can you tell if it's there simply to draw viewers' attention or if it's there because it's a necessary part of the action?" "Does the violence move you in any way to feel compassion? Is the violence more about human suffering and less about blood and gore?" "How was the violent act presented?" "Where was the camera? Are you right in there with the action or are you an observer? Are you the perpetrator or the victim?" "Do hyped-up technical effects distance you from the suffering inflicted? How?"

Discuss emotional violence.

Encourage your child to keep a tally of the types of emotional violence in favorite shows, such as put-downs disguised as humor, verbal threats, or name-calling. Then discuss how emotional violence harms a person and why it can lead to physical violence. Emphasize ways scriptwriters could rewrite verbal abuse and emotional violence to treat human beings with more dignity.

Read about real people who suffered from violence.

Often kids separate violence in movies and video games from real life—yet, when playing violent video games, they rehearse violence and when watching violent films they are thrilled by murder and mayhem. If you bring to your child's attention articles or books about people who suf-

fered from real violence, you can discuss the real consequences of real-life violence, along with the victims' need
for our empathy and compassion.

Predict violent content.

Using any TV schedule, let your child predict which shows
will have violence in them just by reading the titles. Go
through a week's worth of programs and have her choose
the five she considers most violent, explaining the reasons
for the choices. Depending on the age and maturity level
of your child, you can watch a few of the programs with
her to assess the predictions. This is a good activity when
a new TV show, movie, or video game comes out that your
child knows little about. Thinking ahead and considering
what factors would make entertainment violent teaches
important discernment skills.

How do you know what's cool?

Discuss with your child why violent entertainment is often
considered "cool." Some questions to consider are: "What
factors must be included to determine a rating of 'cool'?"
"Who gets to decide what's cool—you, your peers, or the
businesses promoting the violent entertainment?" "Do you
think it's important to be cool? Why or why not?"

AGES FIFTEEN TO EIGHTEEN

Debate your teen.

Teens love an argument. So why not structure a conversation to make it an intentional debate? One topic could be: "Violence on TV and in the movies does (or does not) influence teen behavior." Have your child develop at least five pro or con arguments for this proposal. You do the same, then present the debate at a family gathering. Encourage your teen to discuss this issue with friends or ask his social studies teacher if a debate can be set up in the classroom.

Discuss the value of and problems with rating systems.

Provide opportunities for your teen to admit watching and then discuss movies or TV programs they saw or video games they played that were "off limits." Provide nonjudgmental guidance about what is appropriate viewing for people his age, explaining the reasons why you made this content off limits to him. Include in your discussion the impact of peer pressure for your teen to go against your wishes. What can be done so your teen will honor your wishes and avoid the inappropriate content?

Make a recommended nonviolent TV/video game list for young children.

Have your teen research on the web and through interviews with teachers what TV programs, video games, and even movies are appropriate for younger children. Have her share the lists with preschools and schools in the area or parents your teen may babysit for, or post it on her own blog or website as a community service.

Share and discuss the research.

There are over three thousand reliable research studies linking media violence with real-life violence. Have your teen read one or more of these studies and discuss them with you. Or have him read this book and talk about it with you!

A CHRONOLOGY OF MAJOR FINDINGS, STATEMENTS, AND ACTIONS ON MEDIA VIOLENCE, 1952–2013

Television and entertainment violence and its effects on children have been an issue since the middle of the twentieth century, although you'd barely know it. It seems that every time it captures the national consciousness, usually due to some horrendous act of school violence, it is presented as if it's never been discussed before. Here you will find a chronology of major findings, statements, and actions regarding media violence from 1952 to the present day. Collectively, this places our fight in context, for without understanding the history of this issue, we will forever be starting over when confronting it.

1952 The U.S. House of Representatives conducts the first House committee hearings on TV violence and its impact on children. These are the first of many hearings to occur over the following decades.

1954 The U.S. Senate conducts the first Senate committee hearings on the role of television in juvenile crime.

1961 Federal Communications Commission chairman Newton N. Minow tells the National Association of Broadcasters that American TV is a "vast wasteland."

1969 The National Commission on the Causes and Prevention of Violence cites TV violence as a contributor to violence in our society.

1972 The surgeon general's office issues a report citing a link between TV/movie violence and aggressive behavior.

1975 The National Parent/Teacher Association adopts a resolution demanding that networks and local TV stations reduce the amount of violence in programs and commercials.

1976 The House of Delegates of the American Medical Association adopts a resolution "to actively oppose TV programs containing violence, as well as products and/ or services sponsoring such programs," in "recognition of the fact that TV violence is a risk factor threatening the health and welfare of young Americans, indeed our future society."

1979 Parents of a fifteen-year-old convicted of murdering a neighbor initiate the first known lawsuit against TV networks (*Zamora v. CBS*, et al.), for inciting their son to violence. The suit is unsuccessful.

1982 The National Institute of Mental Health issues an extensive report stating that there is a clear consensus on the strong link between TV violence and aggressive behavior.

1984 The U.S. attorney general's Task Force on Family Violence states that evidence is overwhelming that TV violence contributes to real violence.

1984 Leonard Eron and L. Rowell Huesmann, in a twenty-two-year study that tracked 875 boys and girls from ages eight to thirty, find that those who watched more violent television as children are more likely as adults to commit serious crimes and to use violence to punish their own children.

1984 The American Academy of Pediatrics' Task Force on Children and Television cautions physicians and parents that TV violence promotes aggression.

1985 The American Psychological Association's Commission on Youth and Violence cites research showing a link between TV violence and real violence.

1987 Canadian broadcasters institute a voluntary code on TV violence that discourages broadcasting violent programming early in the evening.

1989 The National PTA again calls for the TV industry to reduce the amount of violence in programs.

1990 The Television Violence Act (TVA) gives three major networks (ABC, CBS, and NBC) an antitrust exemption so they can formulate a joint policy on violence.

1991 Former FCC chairman Newton Minow declares "In 1961 I worried that my children would not benefit much from television, but in 1991 I worry that my children will actually be harmed by it."

1992 The *Journal of the American Medical Association* publishes Dr. Brandon Centerwall's study concluding that "the introduction of television into the United States in the 1950s caused a subsequent doubling of the homicide rate," and "if, hypothetically, television technology had never been developed, there would today be 10,000 fewer murders each year in the United States, 70,000 fewer rapes, and 700,000 fewer injurious assaults."

1992 The American Psychological Association report "Big

World, Small Screen" concludes that the forty years of research on the link between TV violence and real-life violence has been ignored. It goes on to state that the "scientific debate is over" and calls for federal policy to protect society.

1992 Days before the House of Representatives hearings on TV violence, and having been forced to do so by the 1990 Television Violence Act, the broadcast industry releases a set of "voluntary" industry guidelines (called "principles") on violence.

1993 In June, the major TV networks announce their agreement to air parental advisories when shows deemed violent are aired.

1993 The National Council for Families and Television holds the industry-wide Leadership Conference on Violence in Television Programming.

1993 The Departments of Justice, Education, and Health and Human Services sponsor a major conference calling for TV networks to consider the social effects of media violence when designing programming.

1994 The Center for Media and Public Affairs conducts a study of television violence and finds that from 1992 to 1994, depictions of serious violence on television increased 67 percent.

1994 The Entertainment Software Rating Board (ESRB) is established by the Entertainment Software Association.

1997 The first parental guidelines for TV are put into use.

1998 The National Television Violence Study concludes that 60 percent of all TV programs are violent and that "there are substantial risks of harmful effects from viewing violence throughout the television environment."

1998 *Children and Media Violence: A Yearbook from the UNESCO International Clearinghouse on Children and Violence on the Screen* is published. It reviews worldwide studies of media violence from twenty-five countries and outlines the world's concern about the "global aggressive culture" being formed by violent television, particularly violent U.S. television and film.

1999 President Clinton initiates a study by the FTC and the attorney general of the strategies for marketing violent media to children.

2000 Six prestigious organizations that focus on public health issues sign a joint statement endorsing a causal link between media violence and increased aggression in some children.

2001 *Youth Violence: A Report of the Surgeon General* identifies media violence as a contributing factor to youth violence.

2002 A major study by the Parents Television Council finds that violence increased in every time slot on television between 1998 and 2002.

2004 Thirty-nine members of the House of Representatives send a letter to FCC chairman Michael Powell to initiate a "Notice of Inquiry" on the issue of television violence and its impact on children.

2005 Senator Jay Rockefeller of West Virginia introduces S. 616, the Indecent and Gratuitous and Excessive Violent Programming Control Act of 2005. This bill would allow the FCC to regulate, for the first time, violence on cable and satellite programming and violence on regular broadcast television. The measure is referred to the Committee on Commerce, Science, and Transportation, where it dies.

2005 California passes a state law that imposes a civil fine of up to $1,000 on any person who sells or rents a violent video game to a person under the age of eighteen. They define a violent video game as a game in which you "kill, maim, dismember, or sexually assault an image of a human being," and one that a "reasonable person, considering the game as a whole, would find . . . appeals to a deviant or morbid interest of minors" and "is patently offensive to prevailing standards in the community as to what is suitable for minors."

2007 The FCC releases the report *In the Matter of Violent Television and Its Impact on Children*, a report requested in 2004. Among its conclusions is that exposure to violence in the media can increase aggressive behavior in children, and that Congress could limit the hours when violent programming can be broadcast "and/or mandate some other form of consumer choice in obtaining video programming."

2010 A comprehensive meta-analysis by researcher Craig Anderson and his colleagues involving 130,295 participants from around the world finds that "violent video games increase aggressive thoughts, angry feelings, physiological arousal, and aggressive behavior."

2011 The Supreme Court rules that the 2005 California law is unconstitutional and that violent video games are protected by the First Amendment.

2012 The International Society for Research on Aggression issues a statement and research summary on the role of media violence in increasing aggressive actions, thoughts, and feelings.

2013 In the wake of the massacre at Sandy Hook Elementary School in Newtown, Connecticut, President Obama calls for more study of the effects of media violence on our youth.

2013 Media violence is named as one of the top three determinants of youth violence in the National Science Foundation report *Youth Violence: What We Need to Know.*

2013 Senator Jay Rockefeller, chairman of the Senate Commerce Committee, reintroduces the Violent Content Research Act of 2013. Under this bill the National Academy of Sciences would conduct a comprehensive study and investigation of the harmful effects on children of violent video games and violent video programming.

PROFESSIONAL ORGANIZATIONS
THAT OPPOSE MEDIA VIOLENCE

The following organizations have issued strong statements regarding the detrimental effects of media violence based on the significant scientific evidence. While we do not have the room to name every group that has a position statement on media violence, we present here a list of the major organizations. You can visit their websites to read their position statements. And pass them along to your friends!

THE AMERICAN MEDICAL ASSOCIATION (AMA)
330 N. Wabash Ave.
Chicago, IL 60611-5885
800-621-8335
www.ama-assn.org

THE AMERICAN PSYCHOLOGICAL ASSOCIATION (APA)
750 First St. NE
Washington, DC 20002-4242
800-374-2721
www.apa.org

THE AMERICAN ACADEMY OF PEDIATRICS (AAP)
141 Northwest Point Blvd.
Elk Grove Village, IL 60007
800-433-9016
www.aap.org

THE NATIONAL ASSOCIATION FOR THE EDUCATION OF YOUNG CHILDREN (NAEYC)

1313 L St. NW, Suite 500
Washington, DC 20005
202-232-8777
800-424-2460
www.naeyc.org

AMERICAN ACADEMY OF CHILD AND ADOLESCENT PSYCHIATRY (AACAP)

3615 Wisconsin Ave. NW
Washington, DC 20016
202-966-7300
www.aacap.org

NATIONAL PARENT TEACHER ASSOCIATION

1250 North Pitt St.
Alexandria, VA 22314
703-518-1200
www.pta.org

MEDIA LITERACY AND VIOLENCE PREVENTION ORGANIZATIONS

The following is a list of recommended media literacy and violence prevention organizations that you can contact for information.

CAMPAIGN FOR A COMMERCIAL-FREE CHILDHOOD
89 South St., Suite 403
Boston, MA 02111
617-896-9368
www.commercialfreechildhood.org/
CCFC's mission is to support parents' efforts to raise healthy families by limiting commercial access to children and ending the exploitive practice of child-targeted marketing. Their website is an excellent source for advocating on behalf of media literacy education in our schools and homes.

CENTER FOR MEDIA LITERACY
22837 Pacific Coast Highway, #472
Malibu, CA 90265
310-804-3985
www.medialit.org
The Center for Media Literacy (CML) is an educational organization that provides leadership, public education, professional development, and educational resources nationally and internationally. The CML Media Lit Kit provides a vision and directions for successfully introducing media literacy in classrooms and community groups from pre-K to college.

CENTER FOR THE STUDY AND PREVENTION OF VIOLENCE
University of Colorado, Boulder
1440 15th St.
Boulder, CO 80302
303-492-1032
www.colorado.edu/cspv/
The Center for the Study and Prevention of Violence (CSPV)
collects research literature and resources on the causes and
prevention of violence, particularly youth violence. CSPV
produces numerous publications, most of which are avail-
able to download free of charge.

COMMITTEE FOR CHILDREN
2815 Second Ave., Suite 400
Seattle, WA 98121
800-634-4449
www.cfchildren.org/
The Committee for Children is an international nonprofit or-
ganization whose mission is to promote the safety, well-being,
and social development of children by creating quality edu-
cational programs for educators, families, and communities.
The prekindergarten to grade 8 violence prevention curricu-
lum Second Step teaches children prosocial skills and offers
the Bullying Prevention Unit as an add-on program.

INTERNATIONAL CLEARINGHOUSE ON
CHILDREN, YOUTH, AND MEDIA
NORDICOM
University of Gothenburg
Box 713

SE 405 30 Gothenburg, Sweden

nordicom.gu.se/clearinghouse.php

Begun in 1997 as a UNESCO initiative, the International Clearinghouse on Children, Youth, and Media at the University of Gothenburg in Sweden works to increase awareness and knowledge about children, youth, and media. In addition to sponsoring important conferences, the Clearinghouse publishes a compilation of worldwide research on a yearly basis, providing interesting and enlightening information on the impact of media on children from diverse cultures around the globe.

MEDIA EDUCATION FOUNDATION

60 Masonic St.

Northampton, MA 01060

800-897-0089

www.mediaed.org

Directed by well-known media scholar and author Sut Jhally, this foundation produces and distributes award-winning resources for students of media literacy, educators, parents, and community leaders. The Killing Screens: Media and the Culture of Violence and Media Violence and the Cultivation of Fear are exemplary educational videos available based on the groundbreaking work of Dr. George Gerbner.

MEDIA POWER YOUTH

1245 Elm St.

Manchester, NH 03101

603-222-1200

www.mediapoweryouth.org

Media Power Youth collaborates with public health and prevention programs, school districts, and communities to create and implement evidence-based programs with positive results that help parents, professionals, and youth understand media's role in influencing behavior.

MEDIA SMARTS

Canada's Centre for Digital and Media Literacy
950 Gladstone Ave., Suite 120
Ottawa, Ontario, Canada K1Y 3E6
613-224-7721
mediasmarts.ca

Media Smarts is a Canadian not-for-profit organization for digital and media literacy. Its K–12 resources cover a wide range of issues in "traditional" media and also address the unique issues arising for digital media, with classroom lesson plans, worksheets, backgrounders, tip sheets and essays, and multimedia games and quizzes.

NATIONAL ASSOCIATION FOR MEDIA LITERACY EDUCATION

10 Laurel Hill Dr.
Cherry Hill, NJ 08003
888-775-2652
namle.net

NAMLE brings together a broad-based coalition of media literacy practitioners, educators, scholars, students, health care professionals, K–12 teachers, community activists, and media business professionals from diverse fields and professions. The website is an excellent source for free PDFs that define media literacy and describe its core principles.

PARENT COACHING INSTITUTE (PCI)

15600 NE 8th St., Suite B1, #354

Bellevue, WA 98008

888-599-4447

www.ThePCI.org

The PCI works directly with parents to empower them to make daily choices on behalf of their children's optimal cognitive, emotional, and social development. Family support professionals coach parents to deal proactively with media-related issues in their families to prevent Internet and video game addiction.

TAKE THE CHALLENGE

www.takethechallengenow.net

Take the Challenge is a preschool through high school media education program inspired by Stanford University's Student Media Awareness to Reduce Television (SMART) Curriculum, which has shown a reduction in student aggression when implemented. The Take the Challenge program includes lessons that educate students about the effects of excessive media viewing and exposure to violent media. Students also conduct their own research about media use, committed to making changes and educating other students, parents, and community members about the effects of media.

TEACHERS RESISTING UNHEALTHY CHILDREN'S ENTERTAINMENT (TRUCE)

160 Lakeview Ave.

Cambridge, MA 02138

www.truceteachers.org

Teachers Resisting Unhealthy Children's Entertainment is a national group of educators deeply concerned about how children's entertainment and toys are affecting the play and behavior of children in the classroom. Items available for free download include a twenty-page guide, *Facing the Screen Dilemma: Young Children, Technology and Early Education*, as well as toy buying and media action guides.

WHERE TO FIND NONVIOLENT VIDEO GAMES AND FAMILY-FRIENDLY FILMS

CHILDREN'S TECHNOLOGY REVIEW
www.childrenstech.com
Children's Technology Review is a comprehensive search-able review database for children's interactive media. Each product is clearly described and tagged for education content, platform, and age. It is also rated using a standardized rating system. Designed to summarize products and trends in children's interactive media, the publication is modeled on Consumer Reports.

COMMON SENSE MEDIA
650 Townsend, Suite 435
San Francisco, CA 94103
415-863-0600
www.commonsensemedia.org/
Common Sense Media is an excellent resource for movie, TV, video game, and app reviews in addition to media literacy activities for families and educators.

WWW.KIDSITES.COM
KidSites.com proudly announces that it is one of the "oldest sites for kids on the Internet." KidSites has provided reliable and age-appropriate book and movie reviews since 1977.

MICROSOFT FAMILY SAFETY

httpo://foo.live.com/kido/kidoportal.aopx

This portal provides access to kid-friendly cartoons, TV programs, movies, websites, and games, and provides a feature for searching in other languages as well.

PARENTS TELEVISION COUNCIL

707 Wilshire Blvd. #2075

Los Angeles, CA 90017

800-882-6868

http://w2.parentstv.org

PTC is a nonpartisan national organization that advocates responsible entertainment and provides reviews of current television programs and popular movies, along with media literacy resources.

PEACEREAD

http://www.peaceread.org

PeaceRead provides lists of books, videos, and games that support nonviolence.

RESOURCES FOR PROTECTING KIDS ONLINE

CONNECTSAFELY

www.connectsafely.org

ConnectSafely is for parents, teens, educators, advocates, policy makers—everyone engaged in and interested in the social impact of the web. ConnectSafely also has lots of social media and mobile safety tips for teens and parents, the latest family tech news and analysis from NetFamilyNews and SafeKids.com, and many other resources.

NETSMARTZ WORKSHOP

www.netsmartz.org

NetSmartz Workshop is an interactive, educational program of the National Center for Missing & Exploited Children (NCMEC) that provides age-appropriate resources to help teach children and teens ages five to seventeen how to be safer on- and off-line.

WIREDSAFETY

www.wiredsafety.org

WiredSafety is the largest and oldest online safety, education, and support group in the world. Originating in 1995 as a group of volunteers rating websites, it now provides one-on-one help, extensive information, and education to cyberspace users of all ages on a myriad of Internet and interactive technology safety, privacy, and security issues.

ACKNOWLEDGMENTS

We thank our agent, Richard Curtis, for the initiative and foresight to get the ball rolling on a revised edition. We are very grateful to Random House for agreeing, and to Amanda Patten, for bringing her considerable expertise and attentive care to the project.

Many thanks to Dr. Brandon Centerwall, Dr. Don Schifrin, Dr. Craig Anderson, and Dr. Douglas Gentile for taking time to talk with us about their important research so we could bring readers the latest scientific evidence available.

We are very grateful to our supportive colleagues and friends and our families, especially our sainted spouses.

And we thank the thousands around the world who read the first edition of the book, professionals from all walks of life—the military, parent education, law enforcement, academia, medicine, counseling, social work, and education—and offered us unwavering support. You believed and took action. You are true "warriors of the heart." It has been a pleasure and a privilege to walk this path with you.

To each and every one, we extend much gratitude.

May we together continue to make things better for the children we love and for the future we want.

Gloria DeGaetano   *Lt. Col. Dave Grossman*

NOTES

Introduction: It's Not Normal

Adolescents who copy crimes: Wendy Josephson, *Television Violence: A Review of the Effects on Children of Different Ages* (Ottawa: National Clearinghouse on Family Violence, 1995), 40.

"How'd you get here so fast?": Personal correspondence, Dave Grossman (2003).

Chapter One: It's a Violent World . . . For Our Kids

raised in a culture of death: Phil Chalmers, *Inside the Mind of a Teen Killer* (Nashville: Thomas Nelson, 2009), 36.

Equipped with guns, knives, and explosives: http://en.wikipedia .org/wiki/Columbine_High_School_massacre

Harris and Klebold were avid players: Craig Anderson and Karen Dill, "Video Games and Aggressive Thoughts, Feelings, and Behavior in the Laboratory and in Life," *Journal of Personality and Social Psychology*, vol. 78, no. 4, 2000, p. 772.

Doom is widely known as an early example: Sam Rowe, "20 years of Doom: The game that put a gun in your hand," http://www.telegraph.co.uk, December 10, 2013.

"like playing Doom": Chris Berg, "The terrifyingly inscrutable minds behind mass murders," http://www.abc.net.au/un leashed/4150626.html, July 24, 2012.

"straight out of the game": http://en.wikipedia.org/wiki/Doom _(video_game)

"defining the social category of a rampage school shooting": Katherine S. Newman quoted in, "10 years later

Columbine's hold remains strong," Associated Press, http://www.nbcnews.com/id/30259632/ns/us_news-columbine_10_years_later/t/years-later-columbines-hold-remains-strong/, February 27, 2012.

described the shooter as a very angry man: http://en.wikipedia.org/wiki/Sandy_Hook_Elementary_School_shooting

Lanza's dedication to the game: Joseph Bernstein, "Account linked to Adam Lanza reveal shooting game obsession," Buzz Feed, http://www.buzzfeed.com/josephbernstein/account-linked-to-adam-lanza-reveals-shooting-game-obsession, July 1, 2013.

demonstrated his proficiency with headshots: Tracy Connor, "New Mexico teen accused of family slaughter loved 'violent' video games, police say," U.S. News on www.NBCNews.com, January 22, 2013.

thirteen-year-old Noah Crooks: Victoria Taylor, "Father of Iowa teen facing murder charges thought 'I killed Mom accidentally' text was a joke," *New York Daily News* on http://www.nydailynews.com, May 4, 2013.

"copycat of the video game, Grand Theft Auto": Alex Seitz-Wald, "Another kid with an AR-15," *Salon* magazine on www.salon.com, June 10, 2013.

killed two policemen and a dispatcher: Dana Beyerle, "Conviction upheld in 03 Fayette slayings," www.TuscolusaNews.com, February, 18, 2012.

Michael Carneal, the fourteen-year-old: Personal correspondence, Dave Grossman, who was involved in the aftermath and the court cases for both incidents.

"Classroom Avenger" profile of school shooters: http://www.sheppardpratt.org/Documents/classavenger.pdf

an obsession with media violence: Phil Chalmers, *Inside the Mind of a Teen Killer* (Nashville: Thomas Nelson, 2009), 52.

a multiple homicide committed by a juvenile: http://en.wikipe dia.org/wiki/School_shooting

Only eight days after the 1999 Columbine High School massacre: Sam Blumenfeld, "After Columbine: Why School Shootings Still Happen," www.TheNewAmerican.com, May 10, 2012.

killing sixteen before taking his own life: Reach Information Online, http://www.healthcare.reachinformation.com /School%20shooting.aspx

a big fan of violent video games, specifically Counterstrike: Mike Jaccarino, "Training simulation: Mass killers often share obsession with violent video games," www.FoxNews .com, September 12, 2013. http://www.foxnews.com/tech /2013/09/12/training-simulation-mass-killers-often-share -obsession-with-violent-video-games/

Steven Kazmierczak: David Vann, "Portrait of the School Shooter as a Young Man," *Esquire*, August 2008, 116.

caught up in violent video games as youth: Mike Jaccarino, "Training simulation: Mass killers often share obsession with violent video games," www.FoxNews.com, September 12, 2013.

there have been 26 school shootings: John Light, Laura Feeney, and Karen Kamp, BillMoyers.com, "Guns in America, After Newtown, by the numbers," http://www.salon.com /2013/12/14/after_newtown_a_look_at_guns_in_america _partner/December 14, 2013.

He had been playing Grand Theft Auto IV: Paul Szoldra, "8-year-old allegedly shoots and kills his grandmother after playing violent video game," http://www.business insider.com, August 25, 2013.

spend on average forty hours with screen technologies: Victoria J. Rideout, Ulla G. Foehr, and Donald F. Roberts,

Generation M2: Media in the Lives of 8–18 Year-Olds (A Kaiser Family Foundation Study, January 2010), 11.

extraordinary amounts of gruesome content: Caroline Knorr, "Impact of Media Violence Tips", http://www.common sensemedia.org, February 13, 2013.

40,000 simulated murders and 200,000 acts of violence: Joy D. Osofsky, "The Impact of Violence on Children," *The Future of Children*, Vol. 9, No. 3, Winter 1999, 34.

A seminal 2013 study: Matt DeLisi, Michael G. Vaughn, Douglas A. Gentile, Craig A. Anderson, and Jeffrey J. Shook, "Video Games, Delinquency, and Youth Violence: New Evidence," *Youth Violence and Juvenile Justice*, Vol. 11: 132, 2013.

the National Science Foundation issued a comprehensive report: Youth Violence: What We Need to Know," Report of the Subcommittee on Youth Violence of the Advisory Committee to the Social, Behavioral and Economic Sciences Directorate, National Science Foundation, February 1 and 2, 2013, 1.

"today's murder rate would be three times higher": Lt. Col. Dave Grossman, *On Killing: The Psychological Cost of Learning to Kill in War and Society* (New York: Little, Brown & Co., 1996), 301.

the murder rate: Anthony R. Harris, Stephen H. Thomas, Gene A. Fisher, and David J. Hirsch, "Murder and Medicine: The Lethality of Criminal Assault 1960–1999," vol. 6, no. 2, May 2002, 128–66.

The per capita incarceration rate: *Statistical Abstract of the United States*. Washington, D.C.: The U.S. Department of Commerce, Bureau of the Census, editions 1957 to 1997.

the highest incarceration rate in the world: Alex Henderson, "10 ways America has come to resemble a banana republic," *Salon* magazine on www.Salon.com, September 11, 2013.

"averted millions of serious crimes": Lt. Col. Dave Grossman, *On Killing: The Psychological Cost of Learning to Kill in War and Society* (New York: Little, Brown & Co., 1996), 301.

The prime years for violent crime: "Children, Violence, and the Media: A Report for Parents and Policy Makers," Senate Committee on the Judiciary, September 14, 1999, 2.

helping to incarcerate violent criminals: Somini Sengupta, "In hot pursuit of numbers to ward off crime," the *New York Times*, June 19, 2013. http://bits.blogs.nytimes.com/2013 /06/19/in-hot-pursuit-of-numbers-to-ward-off-crime/

were never reported to the police: Seth Stephens-Davidowitz, "How goggling unmasks child abuse," the *New York Times*, July 14, 2013, http://www.nytimes.com/2013/07/14/opin ion/sunday/how-googling-unmasks-child-abuse.html?page wanted=all&_r=0

"factors that make it more difficult to report crime": Seth Stephens-Davidowitz, "How googling unmasks child abuse," the *New York Times*, July 14, 2013, http://www .nytimes.com/2013/07/14/opinion/sunday/how-googling -unmasks-child-abuse.html?pagewanted=all&_r=0

accidental shootings weren't even defined as crimes: Michael Luo and Mike McIntire, "Children and Guns: The Hidden Toll," the *New York Times*, September 28, 2013, http:// www.nytimes.com/2013/09/29/us/children-and-guns -the-hidden-toll.html?ref=todayspaper&pagewanted= all&_r=1&

evolutionary trends over thousands of years: Steven Pinker, *The Better Angels of Our Nature: Why Violence Has Declined* (New York: Penguin Books, 2012).

a disturbing growth trend: David Kopel, "Guns, mental illness, and Newtown," *The Wall Street Journal*, December 18, 2012, http://online.wsj.com/news/articles/SB10001424127 8873237231045781852718574240361

a staggering total of 3,384,000 physical attacks in all U.S. schools yearly: http://bullyingfacts.info/bullying-statistics/

bullied children are at increased risk: R. Kaltiala-Heino, et al., "Bullying at school—an indicator of adolescents at risk for mental disorders," *Journal of Adolescence*, vol. 23, no. 6, 2000, 661–74.

fear of attack or intimidation: National Education Association statistics, in *Bullies and Victims: Helping Your Child Through the Schoolyard Battlefield*, Suellen Fried and Paula Fried (New York: M. Evans and Company, 1996), xii.

One out of every twenty students: http://bullyingfacts.info /bullying-statistics/

students report bullying as a significant problem: http://bully ingfacts.info/bullying-statistics/

have been bullied previously by their peers: http://www.nveee .org/statistics/

"goal was to model the Columbine shootings: Ben Brumfield, Jake Carpenter, and Anne Claire Stapleton, "Prosecutor: Oregon teen planned Columbine-style attack at his school," May, 26, 2013. http://www.cnn.com/2013/05/26 /justice/oregon-teen-bomb-plot/

"I shudder to think what could have happened here": Lauren Hansen, "The echoes of Columbine: A timeline of school massacres and foiled plots," June 3, 2013. http://theweek .com/article/index/244990/the-echoes-of-columbine-a -timeline-of-school-massacres-and-foiled-plots

about the same number have engaged in cyberbullying: http:// www.bullyingstatistics.org/content/cyber-bullying-statis tics.html

leapt to her death: "Rebecca Ann Sedwick suicide: 2 girls ages 12 and 14 arrested for stalking," *Iowa Newsday*, October 15, 2013, http://www.iowanewsday.com/national/17447

-rebecca-ann-sedwick-suicide-2-girls-aged-12-and-14-ar
rested-for-stalking.html

According to a 2008 study from the Yale School of Medicine:
Young-Shin Kim, M.D. and Bennett Leventhal, M.D.,
"Bullying and Suicide: A Review," *International Journal
of Adolescent Medicine and Health,* vol. 20, no. 2, 2008,
133–54.

suicide is the third leading cause of death: "Youth Suicide,"
Center for Disease Control and Prevention, http://www
.cdc.gov/violenceprevention/pub/youth_suicide.html

suicide rates among adolescents have grown: http://www.bul
lyingstatistics.org/content/bullying-statistics-2010.html

a 2008 study of 6,500 children: Keilah A. Worth, Jennifer Gibson Chambers, Daniel H. Nassau, Balvinder K. Rakhra,
and James D. Sargent, "Exposure of US Adolescents to
Extremely Violent Movies," *Pediatrics,* vol. 122, no. 2, August 2008, 306–12.

played by children as young as eight years old: Keilah A. Worth,
Jennifer Gibson Chambers, Daniel H. Nassau, Balvinder K. Rakhra, and James D. Sargent, "Exposure of US
Adolescents to Extremely Violent Movies," *Pediatrics,*
vol. 122, no. 2, August 2008, 306–12.

contains eighty-five acts of verbal or relational aggression per
hour: Sarah M. Coyne, David A. Nelson, Nicola Graham-
Kevan, Emily Keister, David M. Grant, "Mean on the
screen: Psychopathy, relationship aggression, and aggression in the media," *Personality and Individual Differences,*
vol. 48, no. 3, February 28, 2010.

the average children's show contained insults 96 percent of the
time: Cynthia Scheibe and S. Lowery, "Losers, jerks, and
idiots: Name-calling, put-downs, and relational aggression
on TV programs for children and teens," Paper presented

at the Biennial Meeting of the Society for Research on Child Development, Denver, CO, April 1, 2009.

The 2001 U.S. Surgeon General's report: Office of the Surgeon General (US); National Center for Injury Prevention and Control (US); National Institute of Mental Health (US); Center for Mental Health Services (US), *Youth Violence: A Report of the Surgeon General.* Rockville (MD): Office of the Surgeon General (US), 2001, "Chapter 1: Introduction." http://www.ncbi.nlm.nih.gov/books/NBK44297/

saw his mother beaten as well: Tami Abdollah, "John Zawahri's father was abusive, Santa Monica College shooter's mom charged," *Huffington Post*, June 11, 2013. http://www.huffingtonpost.com/2013/06/11/john-zawahri-father abusive_n_3420563.html

main risk factors contributing to violent behavior: Compiled from, Phil Chalmers, *Inside the Mind of a Teen Killer* (Nashville: Thomas Nelson, 2009) and Jun Sung Hong, Hyunkag Cho, Paula Allen-Meares, and Dorothy L. Espelage, "The social ecology of the Columbine High School shootings," *Children and Youth Services Review*, vol. 33, 2011, 861–68.

Like 65 percent of kids in our country: Victoria J. Rideout, Ulla G. Foehr, and Donald F. Roberts, *Generation M2: Media in the Lives of 8–18 Year-Olds* (A Kaiser Family Foundation Study, January, 2010), 12.

An estimated 4 million American children: Ronald Kotulak, *Inside the Brain: Revolutionary Discoveries of How the Mind Works* (Kansas City: Andrews McMeel Publishing, 1996), 89.

more likely to commit violent crimes later in life: Wendy Josephson, *Television Violence: A Review of the Effects on Children of Different Ages* (Ottawa: National Clearinghouse on Family Violence, 1995), 47.

Important protective factors: Compiled from Jun Sung Hong, Hyunkag Cho, Paula Allen-Meares, and Dorothy L. Espelage, "The social ecology of the Columbine High School shootings," *Children and Youth Services Review*, vol. 33, 2011, 861–68.

Chapter Two: The Compelling Evidence

One ship you can ignore, but not an armada: Adrian Raine, *The Anatomy of Violence* (New York: Pantheon Books, 2013), 44–45.

causal connection between media violence and aggressive behavior: Congressional Public Health Summit, July 26, 2000, p. 1. http://www.psychology.iastate.edu/faculty/caa/VGVpolicyDocs/00AAP%20-%20Joint%20Statement.pdf

Dr. Michael Rich: Committee Reports, 108 Congress: 2003–2004: http://thomas.loc.gov/cgi-bin/cpquery/?&dbname=cp108&sid=cp108TVz23&refer=&r_n=sr253.108&item=&sel=TOC_19271&

Jeffrey McIntyre: Lawrie Mifflin, "Many researchers say link is already clear on media and youth violence," the *New York Times*, May 9, 1999. http://www.nytimes.com/1999/05/09/us/many-researchers-say-link-is-already-clear-on-media-and-youth-violence.html?pagewanted=all&src=pm

More children recognized Joe Camel: Elva Arredendo, Diego Castaneda, John Elder, Donald Slymen, and David Dozier, "Brand name logo recognition of fast food and healthy food among children," *Journal of Community Health*, vol. 34, 2009, p. 74.

"The 'causal arrow' in human thought processes": Leonard Mlodinow, *Subliminal: How Your Unconscious Mind Rules Your Behavior* (New York: Vintage Books, 2012), 201.

Mlodinow cites studies: Mlodinow, p. 201.

our unconscious can choose from an entire smorgasbord of interpretations: Mlodinow, p. 203.

The first U.S. Congressional hearings: John P. Murray, "Studying Television Violence: A Research Agenda for the 21st Century," in *Research Paradigms, Television, and Social Behavior*, eds. Joy Asamen and Gordon Berry (Thousand Oaks: Sage Publications, 1998), 370.

television violence was a totally unacceptable risk: John P. Murray, "Impact of Televised Violence," Kansas State University, www.ksu.edu/humec/impact.htm, 1–2.

more violence and cartoons: Newton Minow quoted in E. Barnouw, *Tube of Plenty: The Evolution of American Television* (New York: Oxford University Press, 1975), 300.

as a public health issue: John P. Murray, "Children and Television Violence," *Kansas Journal of Law and Public Policy*, vol. no. 3 (1995), 10.

U.S. Surgeon General issued a warning: Surgeon General's Scientific Advisory Committee on Television and Social Behavior, *Television and Growing Up: The Impact of Television Violence* (Washington, D.C.: Government Printing Office, 1972).

despite the fact that TV violence had increased: C. Mayer, "FCC Chief's Fears: Fowler Sees Threat in Regulation," *Washington Post*, February 6, 1983, K-6.

highest level in twenty years: John P. Murray, "Impact of Televised Violence," Kansas State University, www.ksu.edu /humec/impact.htm, 5.

the causes of the "epidemic of violence": Brandon Centerwall, M. D., "Television and violence: The scale of the problem and where to go from here," *Journal of the American Medical Association*, June 10, 1992, vol. 267, no. 22, 3059–63.

2,500 studies on the effects of TV violence: Pearl D. Bouthilet,

L. Lazar, J. Eds. *National Institute of Mental Health, Television and Behavior: Ten Years of Scientific Progress and Implications for the Eighties, vol. 1,* Summary Report (Washington, D.C.: United States Government Printing Office, 1982).

sales of violent toys had soared more than 600 percent: Levin, Diane, Remote Control Childhood? Combating the Hazards of Media Culture. Washington, D.C.: National Association for the Education of Young Children, 1998, 10.

Television Violence Act: Newsletter from Senator Paul Simon, December 12, 1990.

Children's Television Act: Brian Sullivan, "Children's TV Bill Becomes Law," National Coalition on Television Violence Press Release, December 28, 1990.

shows that served the educational and informational needs of children: Newton Minow and Craig Lamay, "Making Television Safe for Kids," book excerpt in *Time,* June 26, 1995, 70; Cox News Service, "TV Stations Say 'Toons, Reruns Teach Kids," *Bellevue Journal American,* August 30, 1992, B-6.

developed nine contextual features to measure the harmful effects: National Association of Broadcasters "Statement of Principles": Advisory Committee on Public Interest Obligations of Digital Television Broadcasters, "Statement of Principles of Radio and Television Broadcasting," Issued by the Board of Directors of the National Association of Broadcasters, adopted 1990; reaffirmed 1992.

"psychologically harmful" violence is pervasive: George Comstock, "Television Research: Past Problems and Present Issues," in *Research Paradigms, Television, and Social Behavior,* eds. Joy Asamen and Gordon Berry (Thousand Oaks: Sage Publications, 1998), 32.

attracted children to violent programs by alerting kids to their

existence: Federman, Joel (ed.), *National Television Violence Study, Vol. 3, Executive Summary*. Santa Barbara: University of California, 1998, 29–42.

media violence played an important part in increasing aggression: Jo Grobel, "The UNESCO Global Study on Media Violence: Report Presented to the Director General of UNESCO," in *Children and Media Violence: Yearbook from the UNESCO International Clearinghouse on Children and Violence on the Screen*, eds. U. Carlsson and C. Von Felitzen (Nordicom: Goteborg University, 1998), 181–99.

In 1992, Wolfenstein 3D made the victims actually bleed: Douglas A. Gentile and Craig A. Anderson, "Violent video games: The newest media violence hazard," in *Media Violence and Children*, ed. Douglas A. Gentile (Westport: Prager, 2003), 138.

Duke Nukem series: Media Watch Online: "Duke's the King Baby," www.mediawatch.com.

A game called Postal: Susan Nielsen, "A beginner's guide to becoming a video game prude," *Seattle Times*, February 21, 1999, B 7–8.

action figures to go along with violent games: Susan Nielsen, "A beginner's guide to becoming a video game prude," *Seattle Times*, February 21, 1999, B 7–8.

parents never checked the ratings: Douglas A. Gentile, Paul J. Lynch, Jennifer Ruh Linder, and David A. Walsh, "The effects of violent video game habits on adolescent hostility, aggressive behaviors, and school performance," *Journal of Adolescence*, vol. 27, 2004, 5–22.

imitating professional wrestling moves: Dana Candey, "Boy convicted of murder in wrestling death," the *New York Times*, January 26, 2001, http://www.nytimes.com/2001 /01/26/us/boy-convicted-of-murder-in-wrestling-death .html committed a carjacking and shot two other youths, paralleling the film: Douglas A. Gentile and Arturo Sesma Jr., "Developmental approaches to understanding media effects on individuals," in *Media Violence and Children*, ed. Douglas A. Gentile (Westport: Praeger, 2003), 19.

The Parent Television Council: Parents Television Council, "Bloodbath: Violence on Prime Broadcast TV: A PTC State of the Television Industry Report," 1998–2002.

"We don't benefit from ignorance," said Obama: Brett Molina, Obama seeks research into violent video games," *USA Today*, January 16, 2013, http://www.usatoday.com/story/tech/gaming/2013/01/16/obama-gun-violence-video-games/1839879/

"does not mean that everyone is not affected": Douglas A. Gentile and Arturo Sesma Jr., "Developmental approaches to understanding media effects on individuals," in *Media Violence and Children*, ed. Douglas A. Gentile (Westport: Praeger, 2003), 23.

significantly linked to violent behavior: J. Savage, "The effects of media violence exposure on criminal aggression: A meta-analysis," *Criminal Justice and Behavior*, vol. 35, 2000, 1123–36.

"Research on violent television films, and video games": Craig A. Anderson, et al., "The influence of media violence on youth," *Psychological Science in the Public Interest*, vol. 4, no. 3, December 2003, 104.

increased aggressive thoughts, angry feelings, physiological arousal, and aggressive behavior: Craig A. Anderson, et al., "Violent video game effects on aggression, empathy, and prosocial behavior in Eastern and Western countries: A meta-analysis review," *Psychological Bulletin*, vol. 136, no. 2, 2010, 151–73.

"early viewing of violence stimulates aggression": L. Rowell

Huesman, "The impact of electronic media violence: scientific theory and research," *Journal of Adolescent Health*, vol. 41, no. 6, December 2007, 6–13.

Notel: Tannis McBeth Williams, *The Impact of Television: A Natural Experiment in Three Communities* (New York: Academic Press, 1986).

Stanford Study: Thomas Robinson, et al., "Effects of reducing children's television and video game use on aggressive behavior," *Archives of Pediatrics and Adolescent Medicine*, vol. 155, no. 1, January 2001, 17–23.

Seventeen-Year Longitudinal Study: Gina Kolata, "A study finds more links between TV and violence," the *New York Times*, March 29, 2002, http://www.nytimes.com/2002 /03/29/us/a-study-finds-more-links-between-tv-and-vio lence.html

children suffering posttraumatic stress syndrome: "Problems Frequently Caused by Scary Television and Movies," in *Mommy, I'm Scared: How TV and Movies Frighten Children and What We Can Do to Protect Them*, Joanne Cantor (Orlando: Harcourt Brace & Company, 1998), 215.

increased vulnerability to future stressors: Bruce Perry M.D., Ph.D., "Incubated in Terror: Neurodevelopmental Factors in the 'Cycle of Violence,'" in *Children in a Violent Society* ed. Joy D. Osofsky (New York: The Guilford Press, 1997), 124–49.

In a 1999 study: Joanne Cantor, "Media and fear in children and adolescents," in *Media Violence and Children*, ed. Douglas A. Gentile (Westport: Praeger, 2003), 187.

"school fears and social fears arise at this age": Ibid., 189.

a 2006 study: Stacy Smith and Emily Moyer-Guse, "Children and the war on Iraq: Developmental differences in fear responses to television news coverage," *Media Psychology*, vol. 8, no. 3, 2006, 213–37.

"the mean world syndrome": George Gerbner and Nancy Signo-rielli, *Violence Profile, 1967 Through 1988–89: Enduring Patterns*, manuscript. Philadelphia: University of Pennsylvania, Annenberg School of Communication, 1990; George Gerbner, et al., "Growing Up with Television: The Cultivation Perspective," in *Media Effects: Advances in Theory and Research*, eds. J. Bryant and D. Zillmann (Hillsdale: Lawrence Erlbaum, 2009), 17–41.

"media characters often use violence": Brad J. Bushman, Margaret Hall, Robert Randal, "Media violence and youth violence," in Youth Violence: What We Need to Know, Report of the Subcommittee on Youth Violence of the Advisory Committee to the Social, Behavioral and Economic Sciences Directorate, National Science Foundation, February 1 and 2, 2013, 12.

A 1974 study: Ronald Drabman and Margaret Thomas, "Does media violence increase children's toleration of real-life aggression?" *Developmental Psychology*, vol. 10, 1974, 418–21.

In a seminal study in 1978: William Belson, *Television Violence and the Adolescent Boy* (Farnborough, UK: Saxon House, Teakfield Limited, 1978). John P. Murray, "Studying Television Violence: A Research Agenda for the 21st Century," in *Research Paradigms, Television, and Social Behavior*, eds. Joy Asamen and Gordon Berry (Thousand Oaks: Sage Publications, 1998), 387–88.

desensitization prevents the initiation of moral reasoning: Jeanne Funk, "Children's exposure to violent video games and desensitization to violence," *Child and Adolescent Psychiatry*, vol. 14, no. 3, July 2006, 402.

The Wellington, Ohio, tragedy: Cory Zurowski, "Daniel Petric assassinates mom, shoots pastor dad in head over video games," *True Crime Report*, June 14, 2011, http://www

.truecrimereport.com/2011/06/teen_daniel_petric_mur
ders_mom.php

The first *Die Hard* **had eighteen deaths:** Scott Stossel, "The
man who counts the killings," *The Atlantic Monthly*,
May 1997, http://www.theatlantic.com/past/docs/issues
/97may/gerbner.htm

gun violence in PG-13 films has tripled since 1985: Brad Bushman, Patrick Jamieson, Liana Weitz, and Daniel Romer,
"Gun violence trends in movies," *Pediatrics*, vol. 10,
November 11, 2013. http://pediatrics.aappublications.org
/content/early/2013/11/06/peds.2013-1600.full.pdf+html

Dr. Craig Anderson: Radio Interview with Gloria DeGaetano
on Web Talk Radio, *Parent Well in Our Digital World*,
December 23, 2013, http://webtalkradio.net/internet-talk
-radio/2013/12/23/parent-well-in-our-digital-world
-straight-facts-about-media-violence/

four thousand kids try their first cigarette each day: Matthew
Myers, "Let's finish the fight against tobacco," *Huffington
Post*, August 17, 2012.
http://www.huffingtonpost.com/matt-myers/lets-finish-the
-fight-aga_b_1799298.html

Chapter Three: Murder, Torture,
Brutality: Dangerous "Games"

You can kill people until you can't kill them anymore!: Anonymous posting on MetaFilter community weblog http://
www.metafilter.com/127053/Killing-Is-Harmless

Fallout 3, one of the seven top-selling games of all time: Mike
Sauter, *24/7 Wall St.*, March 14, 2013, http://247wallst
.com/special-report/2013/03/14/the-seven-best-selling
-violent-video-games/2/

displays "realistic dismemberment": Fallout 3, Entertainment

Software Rating Board http://www.esrb.org/ratings/synopsis.jsp?Certificate=25545

players can "activate a collar bomb around a slave-woman's neck": Fallout: New Vegas, Entertainment Software Rating Board http://www.esrb.org/ratings/synopsis.jsp?Certificate=29721

sold over 12 million copies worldwide: "Diablo III surpasses 12 million copies sold worldwide," http://www.destructoid.com/diablo-iii-surpasses-12-million-copies-sold-worldwide-244307.phtml

depicts "battles . . . accompanied by slashing and flesh-impact sounds": Diablo III, Entertainment Software Rating Board, http://www.esrb.org/ratings/synopsis.jsp?Certificate=31460

The Godfather: Blackhand Edition: May 17, 2007, http://www.elotrolado.net/hilo_el-padrino-ign-8-0_726374

consumers spent a billion dollars in three days: Eric Bleeker, "GTA 5 sales hit $1 Billion will outsell the entire global music industry," Investor Center, September 28, 2013, http://www.dailyfinance.com/2013/09/28/gta-5-sales-hit-1-billion/

Grand Theft Auto V entered the Guinness Book of World Records: Luke Karmali, "GTA 5 currently holds seven Guinness World Records," October 9, 2013. http://www.ign.com/articles/2013/10/09/gta-5-currently-holds-seven-guinness-world-records

You can't win unless you torture someone: Alex Hern, "Grand Theft Auto 5 under fire for graphic torture scene," *The Guardian*, September 18, 2013, http://www.theguardian.com/technology/2013/sep/18/grand-theft-auto-5-under-fire-for-graphic-torture-scene

talks about the value of using a woman as a urinal: Carolyn Petit,

"City of angels and demons: GameSpot Review of Grand Theft Auto V," September 17, 2013, http://www.gamespot .com/reviews/grand-theft-auto-v-review/1900-6414475/

the player experiences killing animals: Gabriel Winslow-Yost, Purpose-Driven Life, October 6, 2010. http://nplusone mag.com/purpose-driven-life

In 2011, the PC game market grossed $18.6 billion worldwide: "Video game sales wiki." http://vgsales.wikia.com/wiki /Video_game_industry

78 percent of teens have smartphones: Mary Madden, et al., "Teens and technology 2013," Pew Report, March 13, 2013, http://www.pewinternet.org/Reports/2013/Teens-and -Tech.aspx

men, with an average age of thirty, are the largest demographic for violent video games: "2013, Sales, Demographic, and Usage Data: Essential facts about the computer and video game industry," Entertainment Software Association, 2013, http://www.theesa.com/facts/pdfs/esa_ef_2013.pdf

97 percent of twelve- to seventeen-year-olds: Amanda Lenhart, et al., "Teens, video games, and civics," Pew Report, September 16, 2008. http://www.pewinternet.org/Reports /2008/Teens-Video-Games-and-Civics.aspx

90 percent of kids ages eight to sixteen play: Anne Harding, "Violent video games linked to child aggression," CCN Health.com, November 3, 2008. http://www.cnn.com /2008/HEALTH/family/11/03/healthmag.violent.video .kids/index.html?eref=ib_topstories

89 percent of the games are violent: Douglas A. Gentile and Craig A. Anderson, "Violent video games: The newest media violence hazard," in *Media Violence and Children*. ed. Douglas A. Gentile (Westport: Praeger, 2003), 133.

violent content can be found in 98 percent of "teen-rated"

games: K. Haninger and K. Thompson, "Content and ratings of teen-rated video games," *Journal of the American Medical Association*, vol. 291, 2004, 856–65.

labels actually increase the attractiveness of video games for boys and girls of all age groups: Marije Nije Bijvank, et al., "Age and violent-content labels make video games forbidden fruits for youth," *Pediatrics*, vol. 123, March 1, 2009, 870–76.

the growing popularity of Massively Multiplayer Online Role-Playing Games: Andrea Bullock, "The growing popularity of massively multiplayer online role-playing games," Yahoo Contributor Network, May 17, 2006. http://voices.yahoo .com/the-growing-popularity-massively-multiplayer -online-24066.html

"Player Experience of Needs Satisfaction": Scott Rigby and Richard Ryan, *Glued to Games: How Video Games Draw Us in and Hold Us Spellbound* (Santa Barbara: Praeger, 2011), 10.

"when these needs are satisfied": Ibid.

games are remarkably good candidates for need satisfaction": Ibid.

"The . . . headshot is particularly effective in this regard.": In Jamie Madigan, "The psychological appeal of violent shooters," GamesIndustry International, April 9, 2013, http://www.gamesindustry.biz/articles/2013-04-08-the -psychological-appeal-of-violent-shooters

"a strong risk for overuse is present": Scott Rigby and Richard Ryan, *Glued to Games: How Video Games Draw Us in and Hold Us Spellbound* (Santa Barbara: Praeger, 2011), 144.

"vulnerable to an obsessive focus": Ibid., 112

"what the real world doesn't offer": Ibid., 115

personal story of his gaming addiction: Andrew P. Doan and

Brooke Strickland, *Hooked on Games: The Lure and Cost of Video Game and Internet Addiction* (F.E.P International, Inc., 2012).

"seriously damaging multiple areas of their lives": Douglas A. Gentile in Andrew P. Doan and Brooke Strickland, *Hooked on Games: The Lure and Cost of Video Game and Internet Addiction* (F.E.P International, Inc., 2012), 10.

"most pressing public health concern": Hilarie Cash and Kim McDaniel, *Video Games and Your Kids: How Parents Stay in Control* (Enumclaw: Idyll Arbor, Inc.), 2008, xiii.

longer than they intend to play: Douglas A. Gentile and Craig A. Anderson, "Violent video games: The newest media violence hazard," in *Media Violence and Children*, ed. Douglas A. Gentile (Westport: Praeger, 2003), 133.

toddlers and preschoolers interacting with iPads and smart phones for up to two hours daily: Susan Linn, Joan Almon, and Diane Levin, *Facing the Screen Dilemma: Young Children, Technology and Early Education* (The Campaign for a Commercial-Free Childhood and the Alliance for Children, October 2012).

A growing number of children as young as four years old: Victoria Ward, "Toddlers becoming so addicted to iPads they require therapy," *The Telegraph*, April 21, 2013, http://www.telegraph.co.uk/technology/10008707 /Toddlers-becoming-so-addicted-to-iPads-they-require -therapy.html

lower math and school achievement: L. Pagani, et al., "Prospective associations between early childhood exposure and academic, psychosocial, and physical well-being by middle childhood," *Archives of Pediatric and Adolescent Medicine*, vol. 164, no. 5, 425–31.

"That's actually exploitation": "Ethical dilemmas," *The Sydney Herald*, Digital Life, September 20, 2007. http://www

.smh.com.au/news/articles/ethical-dilemmas/2007/09 /19/1189881577195.html

four basic elements that make video games so habit forming: Jane M. Healy, *Endangered Minds: Why Kids Don't Think and What to Do About It* (New York: Simon and Schuster, 1990), 207.

"A definite drug response": Dr. Donald Shifrin, Gloria DeGaetano personal interview, June 22, 1999.

research by Dr. Craig Anderson and Dr. Karen Dill: Craig A. Anderson and Karen E. Dill, "Games and aggressive thoughts, feelings, and behaviors in the laboratory and in life," *Journal of Personality and Social Psychology*, vol. 78, no. 4, 2000, 772–90.

cardiovascular reactions and hostility: Jodi Whitaker and Brad Bushman, "A review of the effects of violent video games on children and adolescents," *Washington and Lee Law Review*, vol. 66, 1038.

"excitation transfer": Andrew Boylan, "Arousal and aggressive response over time: Excitation transfer in graphic video games." Paper presented at the annual meeting of the NCA 94th Annual Convention, TBA, San Diego, CA, December 12, 2013.

"continued exposure to violent videos": Maren Strenziok, Frank Krueger, Gopikrishna Deshpande, Roshel K. Lenroot, Elke van der Meer, and Jordan Grafman, "Fronto-parietal regulation of media violence exposure in adolescents: a multi-method study," *Social Cognitive and Affective Neuroscience*, vol. 6, no. 5, 2011, 537–47. (First published online October 7, 2010.)

a better predictor of a laparoscopic surgeon's skills: J. C. Rosser, Lynch, P. J. Haskamp, D.A. Gentile, and A. Yalif, "The impact of video games in surgical training," *Archives of Surgery*, 142, 2007, 181–86.

video game health learning decreased kids' diabetes-related urgent and emergency visits: Amanda Schaffer, "Don't shoot: Why video games really are linked to violence," *Slate*, April 27, 2007. http://www.slate.com/articles/health _and_science/medical_examiner/2007/04/dont_shoot .html

helped dyslexic kids learn to focus their attention": S. Franceschini, et al., "Action video games make dyslexic children read better," *Current Biology*, vol. 23, no. 6, March 18, 2013, 462–66.

Violent Video Games: Your Child's Favorite Teacher: Douglas A. Gentile and J. Ronald Gentile, "Violent video games as exemplary teachers: A conceptual analysis," *Journal of Youth and Adolescence*, vol. 9, 2008, 127–41.

the firing rate was a mere 15 percent among riflemen: S. L. A. Marshall, *Men Against Fire* (Gloucester: Peter Smith, 1978), 51.

responsible for increasing the firing rate: Ken Murray, Lt. Col. Dave Grossman, and R. W. Kentridge, "Behavioral Psychology," in *Encyclopedia of Violence, Peace and Conflict* (San Diego: Academic Press, 1999).

a direct result of training with simulators: Ibid.

"Violent video games are significantly associated with": Mike Jaccarino, " 'Frag him': Video games ratchet up violence, blur lines between fantasy and reality," FoxNews.com, September 13, 2013, http://www.foxnews.com/tech/2013/09/13 /with-today-ultraviolent-video-games-how-real-is-too-real/

Delroy L. Paulhus: Jan Hoffman, "Everyday sadists among us," the *New York Times*, September 16, 2013. http://well .blogs.nytimes.com/2013/09/16/everyday-sadists-among -us/?src=recg

"our sensibilities as a people": George Drinka, "Mean world, violent world: Are we desensitized to violence," guest

blogger, SheKnows Parenting, January 17, 2013. http://
www.sheknows.com/parenting/articles/981997/are-we
-desensitized-to-real-violence

"how it changes people": Jaron Lanier, *You Are Not a Gadget:
A Manifesto* (New York: Alfred A. Knopf, 2010), 4.

Chapter Four: The Story I Tell Myself About Myself

"identity of the surroundings": Lars Svendsen, *A Philosophy of
Boredom* (Reaktion Books, 2005), 143.

"and I'm never scared anymore": Wendy Josephson, *Television
Violence: A Review of the Effects on Children of Different
Ages* (Ottawa: National Clearinghouse on Family Vio-
lence, 1995), 17–19.

a young child trying to make sense of what terrifies him: Wendy
Josephson, *Television Violence: A Review of the Effects on
Children of Different Ages* (Ottawa: National Clearing-
house on Family Violence, 1995), 32.

exposing children to violent media images is "abuse": Poussaint, Alvin, M.D., "Taking Movie Ratings Seriously: The
Risks Faced by Children Allowed to Watch Films Meant
for Adults Are as Real as Those from Alcohol, Tobacco, or
Abuse," in *Good Housekeeping*, April 1997, 74.

"wishful identification": Brad J. Bushman, Margaret Hall, Robert Randal, "Media violence and youth violence," in Youth
Violence: What We Need To Know," Report of the Subcommittee on Youth Violence of the Advisory Committee
to the Social, Behavioral and Economic Sciences Directorate, National Science Foundation, February 1 and 2,
2013, 12.

"embedded in the child's mind": Jodi Whitaker and Brad Bushman, "A review of the effects of violent video games on
children and adolescents," *Washington and Lee Law Review*, vol. 66, 1038.

"mental processes are thought to be unconscious": Leonard Mlodinow, *Subliminal: How Your Unconscious Mind Rules Your Behavior* (New York: Vintage Books, 2012), 17.

the brain is not fully mature until about age twenty-three or twenty-five: B. J. Casey, R. Jones, and L. Somerville, "Braking and Accelerating of the Adolescent Brain," *Journal of Research on Adolescence* 21 (2011): 21–33.

imitate an array of adult facial features: Brandon Centerwall, "Television and Violence: The Scale of the Problem and Where to Go from Here," *The Journal of the American Medical Association*, vol. 267 (June 10, 1992), 3059.

"They will imitate anything:" Brandon Centerwall, "Television and Violence: The Scale of the Problem and Where to Go from Here," *The Journal of the American Medical Association*, Vol. 267 (June 10, 1992), 3059.

"they have a refrigerator, and there are such things as refrigerators": H. Kelly, "Reasoning About Realities: Children's Evaluations of Television and Books," in *New Directions for Child Development: Viewing Children Through Television*, no. 13, eds. H. Kelly and H. Gardner (San Francisco: Jossey-Bass, 1981), 63.

an Indiana school board had to issue an advisory: Neal Lawrence, "What's happening to our children?" *Midwest Today*, December 1993.

Jerome Bruner: Gloria DeGaetano, "Learning from Creative Play," in *Television and the Lives of Our Children* (Redmond: Train of Thought Publishing, 1998), 35.

"electronic media and their associated toys and artifacts": C. Glenn Cupit, *Play and Quality in Early Childhood: Educating Superheroes and Fairy Princesses* (Melborne: Early Childhood Australia, 2013), 7–8.

children's beliefs about aggression correlate with their aggressive behaviors: N. G. Guerra and L. R. Huesmann, "A cognitive-ecological model of aggression," *Reveue Internationale de Psychologie Sociale*, Vol. 2, 177–204.

the "unique ability to directly increase aggressive cognitions": Brad Bushman, Ibid.

"industry versus inferiority": Erik H. Erikson, *Childhood and Society* (New York: W. W. Norton and Company, 1993), 135.

"Maybe if we cut some of the more violent videogames: quote on the National Campaign to Stop Violence's website: http://www.dtwt.org/the-challenge

middle schoolers play video games more often: Victoria J. Rideout, Ulla G. Foehr, and Donald F. Roberts, *Generation M2: Media in the Lives of 8–18 Year-Olds* (A Kaiser Family Foundation Study, January 2010), 13.

six hours or more each day: Iman Sharif, M.D., and James D. Sargent, M.D., "Association between television, movie, and video game exposure and school exposure," Pediatrics, vol. 118, no. 4, October 1, 2006, 2005–854.

seeing plenty of inappropriate contents: Victoria J. Rideout, Ulla G. Foehr, and Donald F. Roberts, *Generation M2: Media in the Lives of 8–18-Year-Olds* (A Kaiser Family Foundation Study, January 2010), 13.

"most consistent negative impact on school performance": Ibid., 1068.

"limit weekday television and video game time": Ibid., 1067.

A 2001 classic study: Marlene M. Moretti, Roy Holland, and Sue McKay, "Self-other representations and relational and overt aggression in adolescent girls and boys," *Behavioral Sciences and the Law*, vol. 19, no. 1, February 2001, 109–26.

self-efficacy declines in girls during early adolescence: Jeffrey G. Parker, Kenneth Rubin, Stephen A. Erath, Julie Wojslawowicz, and Allison A. Buskirk, "Peer relationships, child development, and adjustment: A developmental psychopathology perspective," in *Developmental Psychopathology, Theory, and Method*, eds. Dante Cicchett and Donald Cohen (New York: Wiley, 2006).

lower feelings of social competence than their peers: Douglas A. Gentile, Hyekyung Choo, Albert Liau, Timothy Sim, Dongdong Li, Daniel Fung, and Ageline Khoo, "Pathological video game use among youths: A two-year longitudinal study," *Pediatrics*, vol. 127, no. 2, February 2011, 319–30.

Brain science of the last two decades: David Dobbs, "Beautiful Brains," *National Geographic*, October 2011, p. 43.

This enabled the shooters: Brad J. Bushman, Margaret Hall, Robert Randal, "Media violence and youth violence," in Youth Violence: What We Need to Know," Report of the Subcommittee on Youth Violence of the Advisory Committee to the Social, Behavioral and Economic Sciences Directorate, National Science Foundation, February 1 and 2, 2013, 12.

Chapter Five: Action Speaks Louder Than Words

"a choice that carries moral weight": Matthew Fox, *Sins of the Spirit, Blessings of the Flesh: Lessons for Transforming Evil in Soul and Society* (New York: Three Rivers Press, 1999), 191.

five essential needs of children: Gloria DeGaetano, *Parenting Well in a Media Age: Keeping Our Kids Human* (Fawnskin: Personhood Press, 2005).

the role of cognitive development: Perry, Bruce, M.D., Ph.D., "Incubated in Terror: Neurodevelopmental Factors in the 'Cycle of Violence,'" in *Maximizing Washington State's Brain Power* (Olympia: Department of Health and Human Services, Fall 1998), 8.

reduces kids' attention span: Edwards L. Swing, Douglas A. Gentile, Craig A. Anderson, and David A. Walsh, "Television and video game exposure and the development of attention problems," *Pediatrics*, vol. 128, no. 2, August 2010, 214–21.

reduce all screen time: American Academy of Pediatrics, Committee on Public Education. American Academy of Pediatrics: "Children, adolescents, and television," *Pediatrics*, vol. 107, no. 2, 2001, 423–26.

not allow television sets in their children's bedrooms: Ibid.

articles on the harmful effects of media violence: Brad Bushman and Craig Anderson, "Weighing the Evidence: Comparison of Two Amicus Briefs Submitted to U.S. Supreme Court Violent Video Game Case, 2011. http://www.psychology.iastate.edu/faculty/caa/abstracts/2010 -2014/11BA.pdf

broad ruling reduced the industry's incentive to police itself: Justice Breyer's dissent in "Brown, Governor of California vs. Entertainment Merchants Association et al.," Supreme Court of the United States, October, 2010. http://www .supremecourt.gov/opinions/10pdf/08-1448.pdf

RESOURCES

A Definition of Harmful Media Violence

Belson, W. *Television Violence and the Adolescent Boy*. Franborough: Teakfield, 1978.

DeGaetano, Gloria, and Kathleen Bander. *Screen Smarts: A Family Guide to Media Literacy*. Boston: Houghton Mifflin, 1996.

Comstock, G., and H. Paik. *Television and the American Child*. San Diego: Academic Press, 1991.

Federman, Joel, ed. *National Television Violence Study, Vol. 3*,

Executive Summary. Santa Barbara: University of California, 1998.

Murray, John. "Children and Television Violence," in *Kansas Journal of Law & Public Policy*, 1995, vol. 4, no. 3, pp. 7–14.

Chronology

Adapted from www.videofreedom.com/chrono.html (Original source: Charles S. Clark, *Communication Quarterly*, September 4, 1993).

Bruce D. Bartholow, Karen E. Dill, Kathryn B. Anderson, and James J. Lindsay, "The Proliferation of Media Violence and Its Economic Underpinnings," in *Media Violence and Children*, Douglas A. Gentile, editor (Westport: Praeger, 2003).

RECOMMENDED READING

Anderson, Craig, Douglas Gentile, and Katherine Buckley. *Violent Video Game Effects on Children and Adolescents: Theory, Research, and Public Policy.* Oxford University Press, 2007.

Baker, Frank. *Media Literacy in the K-12 Classroom.* International Society for Technology in Education, 2012.

Cantor, Joanne. *Mommy, I'm Scared: How TV and Movies Frighten Children and What We Can Do to Protect Them.* Harcourt Brace, 1998.

Cash, Hilarie, and Kim McDaniel. *Video Games & Your Kids: How Parents Stay in Control.* Issues Press, 2008.

Chalmers, Phil. *Inside the Mind of a Teen Killer.* Thomas Nelson, 2009.

Davies, Máire Messenger. *Children, Media and Culture.* Open University Press. 2010.

DeGaetano, Gloria. *Parenting Well in a Media Age: Keeping Our Kids Human.* Personhood Press, 2005.

Doan, Andrew, with Brooke Strickland. *Hooked on Games: The Lure and Cost of Video Game and Internet Addiction.* F. E. P. International, 2012.

Gentile, Douglas A., ed. *Media Violence and Children: A Complete Guide for Parents and Professionals.* Praeger, 2014.

Grossman, Dave. *On Killing: The Psychological Cost of Learning to Kill in War and Society.* Little, Brown, 1996.

Healy, Jane M. *Endangered Minds: Why Our Kids Don't*

Think and What to Do About It. Simon & Schuster, 2005.

Hobbs, Renee. *Digital and Media Literacy: Connecting Culture and Classroom.* Corwin, 2011.

Hoechsmann, Michael. *Media Literacies: A Critical Introduction.* Wiley-Blackwell, 2012.

Kirsh, Steven. *Children, Adolescents, and Media Violence: A Critical Look at the Research.* Sage Publications, 2011.

Mlodinow, Leonard. *Subliminal: How Your Unconscious Mind Rules Your Behavior.* Vintage Books, 2013.

Rigby, Scott, and Richard M. Ryan. *Glued to Games: How Video Games Draw Us In and Hold Us Spellbound.* Praeger, 2011.

Roberts, Kevin. *Cyber Junkie: Escape the Gaming and Internet Trap.* Hazelden, 2010.

Rosen, Larry. *iDisorder: Understanding Our Obsession with Technology and Overcoming Its Hold on Us.* Palgrave Macmillian, 2012.

Sieberg, Daniel. *The Digital Diet: The 4-Step Plan to Break Your Tech Addiction and Regain Balance in Your Life.* Harmony, 2011.

Steiner-Adair, Catherine, and Teresa Barker. *The Big Disconnect: Protecting Childhood and Family Relationships in the Digital Age.* Harper, 2013.

Van Cleave, Ryan. *Unplugged: My Journey into the Dark World of Video Game Addiction.* HCI, 2010.

INDEX

ABOUT THE AUTHORS

LT. COL. DAVE GROSSMAN (U.S.A., ret.) is the author of several books, including the Pulitzer Prize–nominated *On Killing: The Psychological Cost of Learning to Kill in War and Society* and the highly acclaimed *On Combat*. As a West Point psychology professor and professor of military science, Grossman trains medical and health professionals in how to deal with and prevent killing. He trained mental health professionals in the aftermath of the Jonesboro shootings and has been an expert witness and consultant in several murder cases, including those of Timothy McVeigh and Michael Carneal. In the wake of the 9/11 terrorist attacks he has written and spoken extensively on the terrorist threat, with articles published in the *Harvard Journal of Law, Civil Policy*, and many leading law-enforcement journals. Today he is the director of the Killology Research Group. He has been on the road almost three hundred days a year, for fifteen years, as one of our nation's leading trainers of elite military, law-enforcement, and school-safety organizations.

GLORIA DeGAETANO is an acclaimed media-literacy educator and the author of the award-winning book *Parenting Well in a Media Age: Keeping Our Kids Human*. As a consultant and university instructor, DeGaetano has trained thousands of teachers, family-support professionals, and parents in media-related issues since 1987. She originated the parent-coaching profession when she established the Parent Coaching Institute (PCI) in 2000. As CEO of Parent Coach International she directs the Parent Coach Certification Training Program worldwide.

JOIN OUR CAMPAIGN TO
STOP TEACHING OUR KIDS TO KILL

Join us on Facebook at https://www.facebook.com
/Stopteachingourkidstokill.

Here you will find up-to-date information, resources, and current activities taking place around
the globe.

Together we can protect children and teens from
the harmful effects of media violence.

Together we can stop teaching our kids to kill
and to want to kill.